Life of an Intern's Wife

Life, Medicine, Parenthood, and above all,
Love in my Husband's First Year of Residency

Alicia Kwon

Dedication

For everyone who wishes for true love in the real world, for Ko, who has taught me that true love shows up with him when I find the love I seek inside my own being, and for our kids, who uniquely express the Light of the Universe, each in their own extraordinary ways.

~ Alicia

April 19th, 2014

Acknowledgments

Special thanks to Laurel Ornitz for her skillful editing; to Nora and Chana for the ways they saved by sanity during Ko's intern year; to all the baristas, random strangers, teachers, and fellow dancers on life's path who have made me smile through the years; to all the amazing future doctors like Kate and Dylan who are preparing to rock the medical world by bringing healing back into healthcare; to Ko for being unconditional and for teaching me that happiness is an inside job; for my amazing kids who revolutionize my life, open my heart, and inspire me to evolve and open up my being daily; and to everyone who will ever read this book and decide to search out the truth and love in small things, snuggle more often, slide down banisters whenever possible, and take more walks in the park.

Foreword

Those who know Alicia Kwon personally will recognize her wit, insight, and raw transparency, and those who have yet to meet her will get to know her essence poignantly, on the pages of this journal.

Alicia has emerged from the trial of having had a spouse in medical training while raising young children and holding space for her own calling with the kind of grace that embodies her dancing and figure skating. I could not be more lovingly grateful, proud and honored to share in this journey and I am certain you will enjoy partaking in it through the pages of Life of An Intern's Wife!

~ Ko Kwon

Contents

Prologue

One week ago, our silverware, books, beds, multicolored rug of the world, file cabinets, and trophies from childhood rolled away on wheels. I watched the truck as it turned the corner out of our suburban neighborhood in New Jersey and disappeared into a scorching blue day. Now I am on an airplane headed for Portland, Oregon, and there is orange juice on my butt.

My love Ko and I fell for each other three days after I graduated from college with a curly-haired, blonde one-year-old in tow; two days after I officially separated from my ex; and exactly two months before Ko licked, sealed, and mailed his medical school applications. As it happened, my divorce was legal on the precise day that my love started his medical training at the University of Medicine and Dentistry of New Jersey, School of Osteopathic Medicine.

Now, here we are, five years, two more kids later, and Ko has official letters after his name. As for me, I've agreed to go along for this ride, figuring out my own life as I go. You could say the turbulence that led to orange juice on my butt pretty accurately describes what it's been like so far: bumpy, funny, and a little scary.

1

Welcome to Portland

May 29th, 2009

Our plane has just begun its initial descent and we are tired, yet unbelievably excited. We are entering a new land and a whole new chapter of our lives. We rented an apartment from 3,000 miles away. Our new home is about 20 minutes outside Portland proper in a town called Clackamas. It has three bedrooms, a pool, and a hot tub, and places to eat within walking distance. The rent is uncannily cheap too. What's not to love?

When we de-board the plane, we step into an open, airy space. Tall glass ceilings usher in plentiful light, a few feet from us is a children's play area, and a few feet to the left a coffee shop. I could happily live at the airport, I think, as we relax for a few minutes before heading toward baggage claim.

2

Our New Home

May 29th, 2009, Later That Day

We pile our luggage into the back of a checkered cab driven by a kind Lebanese man. The winding highway that takes us to our new pad seems surreal. I don't see any signs of the Greater Portland area I had imagined, full of funky coffee shops and open-minded, semi-hipster, laid-back, socially conscious people. Instead I see power lines towering over island after island of strip mall complexes that look like a child had colored them with a set of Bold Crayola Markers. This looks more like a Walmart sprawl than a "shop local" community. Once we turn into Royal Court Apartments, it takes us a while to locate our unit amidst the many identical-looking carports and pretty landscaping, maintained in greens and pinks. When we finally make it inside the decent, modest-looking apartment, we see that the stove-top area is missing a range hood and there is a faint smell of smoke. I am certain the ashy stench will dissipate once I get around to opening the windows. Fresh air does wonders for cleaning out old odors, so I'm not too worried. Peering around, I find two normal-size bedrooms and an itty-bitty one that looks like a walk-in closet minus the sliding door.

The outdoor landscaping is nice and there is a play area where our almost seven-year-old makes friends right off the bat. Behind the play area are trails ascending a rather steep slope onto a hillside resplendent with ferns and trees. A swimming pool awaits 50 yards from our front door—just a downhill jog and a few skips, and you're in the water. After a quick survey of the land, it becomes clear that our most urgent need is food. Our bellies are gurgling with hunger from a long trip across the country and the mild shock of finding ourselves plopped in unfamiliar territory. The office staff is friendly and actually picks up our stir-fry takeout from down the street, seeing as our car is still traveling through Middle America attached to a truck. We are immensely grateful for this little extra kindness.

Our whole family camps out on the living-room floor, since our beds, along with everything else we own, are probably driving through North Dakota in the dark. I lie awake, trying to find a position that works for sleep. My limbs take turns falling asleep, but I do not.

3

Waking Up

May 30th, 2009

In the morning, a beautiful sunny day awakens us, and we open our windows and sliding deck door when ... YECCHH, cigarette smoke floods the apartment. We rush to close all the doors and windows and planned to hunker down until the smoker had gotten his or her nicotine fix. We spend the next few days opening and closing windows, plotting to find certain times of day that the smokers sleep, go to work, or have some fun out on the town. A cloud of carcinogenic despair descends over us as we come to terms with the fact that if we are lucky, clean air may last one minute, and even then, if we risk opening the windows, there's sure to be a flood of smoke before we can hurry back in time to slam them shut. Sleuthing and surveillance by my husband David (who also goes by the name of Ko) reveals that we are surrounded on all sides by neighbors who do not appear to work, play, or go out at all, except perhaps to buy more cigarettes. Even when we drape blankets over the cracks in our deck and seal off all known air passages, we can still smell the lingering thick scent of smoke, as if it has infiltrated the lungs of the building itself.

But bless the beautiful cherry trees outside our window, as they still proclaim life and vitality in this place. To be fair, there are other signs of life and hope, too. Nika, our oldest daughter, quickly makes friends with a little girl named Taryn, who lives just up a flight of stairs from us. As Taryn's mom carries bags from Costco up the stairs, she says to me, "That girl's always got her face in them books—see?" Sure enough, Taryn is gently holding a library book and smiling.

During the day, we make the best of things, buying an air filter, hosting our cousins from Seattle for a fun visit, inhaling the woody-freshness on the hiking trails behind Crown Court, as though we could get enough clean oxygen in our lungs trail-side to last the whole day. My love and I snap pictures of Gabe and Avriana kissing each other next to a tree stump in the woods. A few days later, we celebrate Nika's seventh birthday poolside, with oregano-drizzled pizza, lemonade, and ice-cream cake.

With our family in tow, my love and I drive into Portland for day trips, and each time we enter the tree-dotted streets of the city, a happy feeling comes over us. Our kids seem happy on these excursions too. Still, it seems untenable to move a family of five into an urban living situation.

"If it were just the two of us, wouldn't it be so cool to spend a year or two living in the city?" One or the other of us says it at least once or twice a day, wistfully. It's not a wistful longing to get rid of the kids we love, but a wishful ache to participate in the lifeblood of the city, where our own pulse seems to resonate.

One day, an earth-shattering insight occurs to me. As the thought forms, I turn toward my love and say:

"If we wanted to live in the city, maybe we would want to live downtown. What if we screw the in-unit washer and dryer, forego our own bedroom, lose another 10 pounds of nonessential furniture and stuff, and just make a two bedroom work? Sure most young professionals move *out* of the city when they have a kid, or at least by kid number two. Let's defy convention and move *into* the city."

Of the two of us, I'm the more idealistic, head-in-the-clouds one, and he is the more earthy, pragmatic one, who actually pictures what will happen to five peoples' worth of laundry if we don't have an in-unit washer and dryer. And were it not for the smoke, and the fact that the only other person in our neighborhood who seems to like books as much as we do is a seven-year-old girl, we probably wouldn't have aligned on the idea of saying goodbye to the little luxuries of suburbia, but desperation sets our minds and hearts on the same page.

"I think you're right, Alicia. Let's do it" was the instant response of my spouse. At the time we were driving down I-5, with the kids in the back. Were it not for that, I could have bedded him right there and then. Few things are as attractive as a shared vision in a time of decision.

4

The Pearl

June 17th, 2009

Two and a half weeks later, we officially break our lease, scrub the apartment within an inch of its life in a semi-futile attempt to recoup our deposit, and turn in the key. We say farewell to the pool, the hot tub, the hiking trails, the smoke, the nearby strip malls, and the smiley seven- year-old girl who loves to read.

With the help of a few good men, we load a U-haul truck and head for Lovejoy Station, an affordable-housing building that you would never recognize as subsidized housing, either from its looks or its location in the loveliest section of Portland's Pearl District. The only true giveaway is the diversity of those who occupy this building. Among the eccentric residents, one of my favorites is Steve, a sixtyish bachelor who is often seen in shimmering purple shorts. In earlier chapters of his life, Steve was chemist and a professor. He loves to discuss history and philosophy, often on the way to the laundry room, in his purple shorts.

Across the street from our new home is a state-of-the-art urban park with a fish pond with lily pads, grass-covered steps, and meandering gravel trails running parallel to a bubbly brook that flows over natural stones. In the distance is a stunning view of the Fremont Bridge. You can see little cars that look like toys coming and going across the Fremont's graceful arch. It looks like a scene from the introductory credits of a sitcom.

In the office downstairs, we meet the part-time office manager, Bob, who is in only on Saturdays and is one of the sweetest people on earth. A few of the other residents are chatting about rumors that Harrison Ford is in town shooting a film.

Instead, on our first night at Lovejoy Station, a Toyota commercial is being shot outside our window. It's ironic to see a big truck pouring water over the street in a town that only has dry streets a few months out of the year. The chic Toyota careens smoothly up and down the street, meticulously turning the corner from 10th Avenue onto Northrup, occasionally stopping for real traffic. Our troupe of five gathers at the window to listen as some guy, probably from California, says, "Take Two." He really says that, outside our window, with cold, theatrical lights shining as if our street were really a stage. It all seems excessively glamorous for a commercial shoot. I can't help laughing out loud at our own gawking wonder. Why unpack when you can watch a commercial outside your window? The irony is, since we only use our TV for flicks, we don't watch commercials *unless*, like tonight, they happen to be showing live outside our window. I never would have imagined it could be so much fun watching a sporty Toyota driving in fake rain.

5

Internship, Day One

July 1st, 2009

I roll out of bed early and get my Flip video camera in time to film my love brushing his teeth in his boxers. A month or so ago, he got special letters after his name. Today he starts being a doctor, or at least being expected to be one. My love's first rotation is Maternal Child Health, which is usually just called OB, but includes, along with monitoring labors and delivering babies, doing pediatric admissions, as well as caring for infants in the nursery. What a lot to do for a brand-new doctor who has no idea what the heck he is doing!

There is something about the demarcation of the person my husband is at this moment, preparing for his first day at work, and who he will be when he comes home that makes me think about losing one's virginity. It's like you know something important has changed in your status, and maybe in your psyche, but can other people tell? Do you walk around differently, smell differently, communicate a different air to the world? Or is it all in your head? Or is it a significant but less than mind-blowing milestone on the journey of life, like purchasing your first (legal) alcoholic beverage or swiping your own credit card for the first time? Will I recognize my husband when he comes home to me after this initiation into doctor-hood, or will there be something intangibly unfamiliar in his stride?

At about 6:20 in the evening, a key wiggles and jiggles in the door, until finally it opens, letting in a young doctor who looks a little goofy and dazed, like he has just walked through a maze blindfolded and somehow survived to get let out on the other side, at least for today. He is both familiar and unfamiliar to me.

I hug this young doctor, who is my husband, and we kiss. Within seconds, the kids attach themselves to their daddy's legs. I can tell my love is happy to be home, though he looks a little like someone who has finished a long race: relieved, exhausted, and on the verge of physical collapse.

I try not to pry, to give him space to be, to process, to not have to explain or talk. Eventually, totally curious, I ask, "So, how was your first day?"

"Well, I made it through."

He mumbles a few additional words: "Women. Labor. Cervix Checks. Bilirubin."

"I asked a lot of questions because I really had no clue what I was doing."

It seems he didn't inadvertently kill any mothers, infants, or children, and like he said, he made it through.

6

First Call

July 4th, 2009

For the kids and me, July 4th is just another day. It's not a freebie family day, since it is my love's first night on-call, following a typically long workday. To tell you the truth, Independence Day hasn't been a big deal since I sat on the lawn of my hometown watching fireworks with a couple from the church I went to. It was two months before my first wedding. Sitting on that grassy hill, the couple from church asked me if I was sure I wanted to go through with the marriage. I lied and said "Yes" in blatant opposition to my own inner truth. I had been warned, from the outside and the inside, and still somehow I made myself go through with it. Why do we make ourselves do things we don't even want to do when we know it's bad for us?

Was it pride? Fear of admitting I was wrong? Insecurity about facing the unknown adult world alone? I was 19 that Fourth of July.

Ten years later, I'm standing at the edge of Tanner Springs, watching my three children careen around the wide sidewalks that frame the park into a square, riding scooters my mom had shipped to us a few weeks ago. It fascinates me to observe the way they ride expresses their unique ways of being in the world.

Nika rides with a combination of grace and flare. Her essence is like the innocence of an angel, and she has this crazy sense of style, creativity, and humor. I wonder who she would be, if she would be, if I hadn't married her biological dad. I'm convinced her soul saw the situation and the open opportunity for incarnation and said something like "Hey, I'm flexible," went with the detour, entered an unexpected, yet lovely body, and showed up earlier, probably with a different hair color and outward personality pattern than if I had waited to have her later in life.

Off doing his own thing, Gabe meanders on his scooter in zig-zag patterns like the absentminded professor, while Avriana scoots with a passion and speed incomprehensible for the tiny package she currently occupies.

Like Gabe, my thoughts wander. I wonder what other people are doing this Fourth of July. Then I wonder if I am at all proud to be an American, and if national pride is good or bad or neutral.

At first I can't think of anything about being an American that makes me feel proud. I'm not ultimately impressed with our nation for having fought an entire war over a tea tax. Canada and India got their independence through persistence, diplomacy, and peaceful noncompliance. We had to fight for independence with bayonets and blood, and it seems that while we wanted fair representation, we also wanted greater freedom, though denying the same rights to the people who were here first. I'm not proud of the United States' poor rankings on every well-being index compared with other industrialized nations, or its consumptive addiction that has gotten us into the most complicated economic and environmental crisis imaginable.

I try to remember the things I *can* be proud of being an American, because I feel like at least there ought to be a healthy balance of critique and affirmation. I go down the list: our public education ... nope, our treatment of the poor and elderly ... nope, our political integrity ... nope, our healthcare system? Heck no.

Finally I remember an observation from a lovely French woman I met a couple of years ago because she married my ex-husband. I couldn't ask for a kinder, more wonderful stepmother or friend for my oldest daughter, and I'm thrilled that she showed up and the two of them fell in love. My ex's wife and I were talking one day and she was saying things like "I can't stand France. I hate it because there if you have an entrepreneurial idea or an inspiration outside the parameters of 'the system,' your friends and relatives will tell you, 'Come on, it's never going to happen.' But here in the United States people are really supportive if you have an idea of something you want to do."

I had totally taken that aspect of America for granted. Our small businesses may have a high failure rate, but at least we have the freedom to dream, to dare, and to do what inspires the hell out of us.

As time passes and the day ambles by uneventfully, I also wonder what's happening at the hospital where my love is doing whatever it is he does. I wonder if he feels like a real doctor answering pages, or if he's faking it till he makes it. In the evening, I put the kids to bed as usual. I listen alone to the distant sounds of fireworks until the crackles subside into the night and I lay awake, staring at the ceiling. I get up and push the kids' scooters in front of the door like a blockade just in case someone knows I'm home alone with the kids tonight and decides to try to break in. I figure if they start to open the door and something metal and loud makes a big noise, it'll be more likely to scare them off.

Eventually daylight comes. I think I slept a few minutes, and it appears no one attempted a break-in, a good precedent considering how many lonely nights are up ahead.

I drop the kids off at preschool and head home to do some work, and around 11:20, a haggard, sweet-looking man walks in the door and stretches out his arms toward me.

"How'd it go?" I ask.

"Well, Alicia, it was, well, quite interesting." It turns out "interesting" included an overweight-looking woman who came in for cramps, back pain, and diarrhea. Her diagnosis? Labor. My love recounts to me, over a snack of cashews at the counter, how he inquired, "You didn't know before today that you are nine months pregnant?" She said, "No, I never thought that was it."

At a certain point, the nurses failed to find the baby's heartbeat and started freaking out.

"How do we tell this person she is having a baby *right now*?" turned into "Oh my, someone will have to counsel the patient about possible fetal demise." That job seemed to be landing squarely in the lap of the new intern, aka, my husband. "Dr. Kwon, how are we gonna tell this lady she may be losing the baby she just found out she is having?" Eventually, fetal heart tones were found, and the baby actually came out fine and was whisked off to the nursery. The very surprised mother admitted that "she made a mistake" and vowed to use birth control in the future. Nobody even knew the identity of the father—the patient kept this knowledge to herself. The baby was destined for adoption, hopefully to a loving home. As for the new intern, he was chastised for calling too many people for help. Like he should have known that if the senior resident says, "No, I don't want to help you handle this," you're supposed to tell them, "Okay, so help me anyway, even if you don't want to," instead of calling the on-call attending physicians.

The rest of my love's first night included a six-year-old with trouble breathing, babies with sky-high bilirubin, giving the wrong dose of an antibiotic to someone, facing a tricky decision over whether or not to place misoprostol in a woman's cervix as part of her labor induction, admitting a woman with suspected placental abruption who turned out to be having totally normal braxton hicks contractions, and fumbling through seemingly esoteric admissions forms.

It seems my love had been put through the ringer and came out alive, just like the surprise baby he helped deliver.

7

The Night Watch

September 12th, 2009

It is funny how people, especially little people, emulate the rhythms of the ones they love, even from a distance. Gabe and Avsi, without fail, wake up at least five times a night when their father is on-call. This Friday evening is, unfortunately, not turning out to be an exception.

Avsi awakens in fowl moods at 12, 1, 2, and 4 a.m., respectively. Of course, in learning to ride the waves, I've finally learned to give her space until she calms down enough to be receptive to affection and comfort. I imagine that when she is upset, her skin and insides crawl with outrageous sensitivity, so that while she wants to escape her internal suffering, she also can't stand to be touched, or to have another's energy invade her space. I remember feeling like that during labor. Usually a total hugger, in labor, touch made me angry.

I wish my little one would just let me scoop her up and hug her and tuck her happily back in bed, but every time I'm faced with this sort of insanity, this waking up to endless screaming, I find myself teetering between resistance and wishing. With resistance, I'm on the edge of becoming the sort of parent people call social services about. A wish, on the other hand, has a softness to it. A wish opens the heart, whereas resistance slams it shut. I wish comfort for us both.

Just when it seems Avsi is winding down, she becomes upset once again, but like the tide slowly going out, every time the waves roll in and out, the water slowly recedes. With waves of feeling, I watch Avriana inch closer to peace, then back off from it, and then turn toward it ever more so. Eventually with arms outstretched, she says definitively, yet softly, "Pick me up." I hold her gently, yet firmly, aching with tiredness and tenderness, wondering when she'll outgrow this phase, wondering if she is fragile or tough. The truth is, like all of us, she is both fragile and tough, sensitive and strong. She is just more of both than the average person.

Having finally won Avriana's trust, I venture with her in my arms to the window, where we watch the street below shifting through its nighttime cycles. Strangers passing by in fancy coats alongside dogs on white leather leashes. Cars passing on their way to here or there. A party, maybe? A guy yells something. Who knows if he is talking to another person, or talking to himself. Night passing into the navy-blue hour just before morning. The city quiet except for a lone man walking his dog like it's the most normal thing to do at this hour. I coax us into bed and we sleep, snuggled into each other for an hour or so, in which there is nothing to wish for at all. I have everything.

Gabe wakes up at 5:45 a.m. I wonder if my son is emulating his father, waking up now too, as he prepares to see his patients in morning rounds.

8

What You Can Learn About Doctors from a Turkey Sandwich

September 12, 2009

It's Saturday morning and rain is falling gently outside the window. In spite of its ubiquitous presence, on the whole Portlanders frown on the perpetuity of fall rain. I like it. It has a comforting, soft feeling, washing old things away, easing the day's rhythm into a slower pace. My love will probably be home around 10 this morning, after a Friday-night on-call shift. In the meantime, Nika is completely absorbed in one of her new books, and Gabe and Avsi decide to get decked out in pink and green raincoats for a trip downstairs and out into the rain.

We greet the potted plants that stand on either side of Lovejoy Station's entrance like flowery sentry guards. I snap the cutest picture of the two kids laughing and jumping in the rain, having imaginary conversations with the plants.

We head inside and call the grandmothers: Nana (my mom) and Nanook (my love's mom, who was bestowed with her unique title by Nika at the age of 20 months). Calling the grandmothers is a highly popular activity. Everyone clamors for a turn on the phone, while I daydream ahead to the hour when my wonderful husband will be home and I will be ... out. It will be an effortless hour of easy reading, which is almost as nice as peaceful sleep, even though I can't quite recall how it feels to enjoy the latter.

The grandmother talks wind down, and at half past 9 or so, my favorite intern walks through the door. I'm the first to hear the key jiggling the lock. I sneak over, ahead of the kids. A long and wondrous hug ensues between two very tired people who are extremely pleased to see each other, even as they stagger a bit from the dazed feeling of working hard and sleeping little.

The moment the kids find us and join the hug, our entire family turns into a pile. My love and I lie there for a while, letting the kids climb all over us, and eventually we shake off the daze enough to gather around the table for a late-morning smorgasbord of the buckwheat cereal I prepared earlier, some random pieces of fruit, and a unique contribution from my love: a turkey sandwich with one large bite taken from each half.

It seems a few days ago when my love was on-call it occurred to him to grab a turkey sandwich from the cafeteria to save for later. My love labeled the plastic wrapping with his name in black permanent marker and stashed it in the fridge of the physician's lounge for when he had a moment to nosh. Eventually he got hungry, after gosh knows how many pages, rounds, and admissions, but when he went to get that turkey sandwich, instead of enjoying it with due thanks, he found that someone had stolen it, in spite of the black permanent marker indicating the sandwich was claimed. Mind you this was in the *physician's* lounge.

As our whole family leans in, my love reports what happened during the on-call shift he just got back from:

"This time I set aside *two* sandwiches and I took huge bites out of *both* of them. Someone STILL took one of them."

I had no idea docs were so desperate.

9

Stop Compressions

September 19th, 2009

Sitting around our child's-size table eating buckwheat cereal (now room temperature), my favorite intern tells me about a cancer patient with an exceptionally poor prognosis. Apparently the oncologist gave him a few weeks. My husband, brilliant man that he is, looked at the patient and gave him less than a day. If the oncologist's opinion had won, the patient's family may never have had the opportunity to say goodbye. The family was there with him, thankfully. They were there because my husband called them in. He is as empathetic as he is brilliant, which is why I have said, since I first met him as a medical assistant, that I would choose him for my doctor completely apart from any personal bias.

So the patient's family, a chaplain, and my husband were all there with him when he transitioned to the next thing after life. That transition was almost unnecessarily turbulent. Here's why: The patient had not signed a DNR (do not resuscitate) order. In his case, pounding his chest, puncturing his neck, and shoving plastic tubes down his throat would have done nothing to help his cause. His family unanimously agreed that he would want to go peacefully and that he wouldn't have wanted extraordinary measures taken. In fact, months earlier, the patient had declined a surgery that could have prolonged his life, arguing that he didn't want to go through a major surgery only to hold at bay the inevitable. Yet, when death was staring him in the face, he insisted he wanted everything done, crash cart and all, even if it wouldn't make an ounce of difference. Who can blame him? I can imagine doing the same thing if I suddenly were faced with imminent termination.

Calling in the Ethics Committee, it was decided that since extraordinary measures would offer no clinical benefit, the patient's team, at the appropriate time, officially agreed that it would be best to let nature take its course without interference. When the time came, the nurse, as per the patient's wishes, began compressions and an airbag was placed on the patient. The family medicine team was called into the room, and after concurring once again, officially, that a full code would not help the patient's chances, my husband softly said, "Stop compressions." I'm sure he said it with the utmost compassion and gentleness. I'm sure of this because that's who my husband is as a human being. The only thing is, apparently my love's kind voice was so soft that it was drowned out by machines and air static. "You have to say it louder," nudged an attending nearby. Feeling jarred, my husband bellowed, "STOP COMPRESSIONS!" at the top of his lungs.

Life is about finding the balance point, and then finding it again when it shifts, moments later. It takes practice to continually occupy the invisible center from which truth spoken in love is loud enough to hear and soft enough to be understood.

10

I Love Ortho

September 21st, 2009

In the morning my love and I wake up to various smallish creatures climbing all over us in bed. It is hard to tell how many arms and legs there are in all, and to whom each limb belongs. It is hard to breathe, because someone's little butt is bouncing on my face, squishing my nasal passages more or less shut. Gabe is imagining he is a kitten, offering up soft nuzzles and what has to be one of the most convincing meows to emanate from a non-feline being. If you had your eyes closed, you may have thought there really was a plaintively meowing cat in the house. The fact that little beings are crawling on my body parts in the early morning is ordinary. What is out of the ordinary is that there is another adult in bed with me, spooning me from behind and nuzzling me and periodically grunting when one of the littler family members happens to inadvertently jut an elbow into his ribs in the course of their wiggling.

I'm thinking about why I actually have a man in bed with me, and I look outside and sure enough, there is daylight. How odd. Is he late? Did he forget he's an intern and he's supposed to be at the hospital at 5:30 or 6 at the latest? Then it occurs to me, it's ORTHO! Orthopedics is one of those intern rotations understood to be fairly chill. As a family doc, it's not as if you're expected to saw off any necrotic leg or take the finger Johnny accidentally sliced off with his X-Acto knife out of a plastic baggy and sew it back on straight. Family doctors mostly manage blood pressure and colds, reassure worried parents, sign various forms, prescribe and tweak medicines for chronic issues, and apply the best "evidence-based" treatments to fend off encroaching disease processes. They don't do that much with bones other than order tests and maybe do an occasional splint, so there isn't too much to do on an ortho rotation for a family practice intern other than follow the orthopedist around and take in the scenery of X-rays and MRIs.

I am incredibly chill with this idea of a couple of weeks that seem less like a swim-or-drown educational situation and more like old-fashioned job shadowing.

Recently I hired a local college student to come in the mornings to help the kids prepare for school. My oldest who is not biologically designed for school starting anytime before 9:30 a.m. is less resistant to waking up with a sitter than with me, and I find it helpful to have someone else feed and dress the little ones, at least for this season, otherwise I am utterly worn out by 8:15 from dealing with multiple morning tantrums and meltdowns over petty preferences that take on do-or-die proportions. I'm talking about full-on, flat-on-the-floor writhing tantrums that occur when Avsi adamantly wants me to pick out her undies, yet cannot stand, literally cannot stand, the ones I pick out, even if I pick out two of three options. Ten minutes into it, I find out that what she wants is one particular pair of pink undies that are in the laundry basket with a poop stain or a specific shirt that is sopping wet from lying next to the tub during a bath. This is a girl with a will so strong she will try to put on the poopy pink undies or the water-logged shirt once she has set her mind to what she wants.

Typically, Gabe doesn't like any of his food and has an impressive capacity to whine incessantly, while fiddling with his spoon. It seems like he is intent on honing his skills to perform a Concerto in F Major, with F standing for Fussy.

I can be intense for sure, but generally I'm a pretty rational person, even in a fit of rage. My first sentences were rational negotiations, leading my parents to project a future in law. But these little beings who shared my body, and now my house and heart, seem to latch onto entire worlds of irrationality in which they invest every inch of their enormous willpower. I don't know if this is idiosyncratic, normal, insane, or what, but here's what I know: I wish we could spend more of our time having fun, expressing love, and experiencing more of what life has to offer than the conflict-ridden sock drawer.

So, for less than some people spend on clothes per week, I hired a lifesaver. When Hannah is not saving my life by watching my kids and helping to organize my kids and my house, her other job is researching how to save other people's lives as a neuroscientist looking at how to reverse stroke damage. Hannah and her husband are both scientists. They have their own lab, where they conduct experiments on the weekends, while they wait for full-time funding to come through. Hannah's husband doesn't want kids, and Hannah is at peace with that, yet at the same time she has a soft spot for children. For her, being a nanny is a way for her to connect with kiddos that fits with her life and her relationship. Another fabulous thing about Hannah is that she loves to clean and does so, on instinct, wherever she goes. I wasn't born with that instinct. I was only born with an instinct to make piles.

In college, I was known for the messiest room and the tallest piles. I still got A's and A-minuses, with the occasional B. My only C was in drama class, because I highlighted something in the wrong color pen, which apparently was an important part of the expectations. Since I have never cared about arbitrary expectations that don't make sense, the drama class incident did not motivate me to change my unclean ways. It's true that had I paid more attention to those assignment instructions, I may have avoided tainting my academic record for all posterity with that one intrusive C. But the sheer ridiculousness of getting a C in an acting class because of using the wrong color highlighter seemed so unfair and absurd and funny, it made me more rebellious toward anything smelling institutional, including personal organization and basic household cleaning. Dishes be damned, if I had to pick between spending 30 minutes in dirty soapy bubbles to clean a space liable to get just as dirty the next day, and reading an interesting, uplifting, or enlightening book. Even when I was pregnant, I didn't have a strong cleaning instinct. With my oldest, I nested by finishing a zillion papers and projects in order to finish my junior year of college in time for Baby Nika's early June arrival. With the middle one, I nested by trying to fix a Presbyterian church. They implemented a few of my suggestions a few years after I left the church. With the youngest, I spent hours banging nails into walls and hanging paintings with an exactitude for perfect angles unknown to me before or since that time.

In any event, Hannah has come into our lives, and I would say that she is an answer to prayer, but I don't think she believes in prayer. She is an ethical humanist. So maybe I can at least say that she is a source of goodness and a bringer of comfort and joy and help, which is thankfully received.

Nika's carpool buddy peers around the door and says, "Come on Nika, it's time to go. I have to get to school for play rehearsal." Nika has finally pulled a new shirt over her head and flung her backpack over one shoulder. Her ponytail is still the one from yesterday. "Mom, can you do my ponytail, please?" she asks. I twist a fresh turquoise elastic into her hair and give her a hug as she tromps off with her carpool buddy. "Have a wonderful day!" I call out, as the two girls flip-flop their way down the hall.

Then I turn to my love and we exchange a look. He has one word for me: "Banister?" I slip into sneakers and my love dons orange flip-flops. With about 4 minutes to hang out, the two of us set out for Tanner Springs.

To the left of the park's grass-covered steps is an ordinary stairway leading down to the fish pond. The concrete stairway is divided into two sides by a double railing, which is grayish silver and smooth, in the way pewter is smooth, but not too smooth. Whenever my love and I have a few moments—no less, no more—it has become tradition to make for the banister at Tanner Springs. It takes only seconds to glide from top to bottom, one after another, or together, and the thrill lasts all day.

"Want to slide down?" inquires my love.

"YES " I say.

He likes to face sideways. I like to straddle the banister and slide down forward. Traveling as one, we make something like an L. At the bottom, we slip off the railing, with a feeling of being impressed with ourselves and in love at the same time. We kiss goodbye and he's off in his pale greenish-blue scrubs, running 2 minutes late.

11

Interviewing Preschool

September 21st, 2009 (Later)

I head for Urban Grind, a green coffee shop a few blocks up, on 14th Street. I think they try to be ecologically conscious and socially conscious, but when I say it's a green coffee shop, I mean it literally. The walls are the color of lime-green tropical leaves, and there is weird art on one wall. Something along the theme of if Georgia O'Keeffe and Matisse got high together.

I have an hour to focus my thoughts for the day, read, and sip chai before I take Gabe and Avsi to look at a preschool I'm falling in love with, as surely as I love that guy I slid down the banister with a few minutes ago. I'm a pretty efficient shopper, and after scanning 15 pages of Google listings, I think I have found the one. I certainly hope so, because like finding a life partner, the choice you make in a preschool will influence a future you cannot yet imagine.

After my chai, I walk home to collect the kids from our overqualified sitter who has even printed out directions for me to our much anticipated trip to check out Overlook Collaborative Preschool. I maneuver Gabe and Avsi into their car seats. It takes at least 5 minutes, between negotiating seating preferences and last-minute needs for this or that book or snack or stuffed animal to hold. At last we leave the garage and off we go to North Portland.

As we pull into the driveway of Overlook, an entourage of sunflowers greets us, bobbing over a wooden fence, as if beckoning us to enter. The teacher, Erin, is as lovely as her voice on the phone, with a mile-wide smile, and a seamless intertwining of professionalism and giddiness ideal for a preschool teacher. "I'm a big three-year-old," Erin confesses, as she excitedly tells me about all the fun they have at the school. Gabe and Avsi fit simply and naturally into the surroundings. Within minutes, they are smocked and painting watercolors in rainbow hues.

Infatuation is effervescent feelings percolating from your brain to your toes, but from time to time it is the harbinger of falling in love with the very essence of life itself. So it is with the little preschool we find. The teacher, Erin, has, with the help of her handy husband, created a wonderland out of their North Portland cottage. The school effuses with expressions of their love for each other and the kids they envisioned blossoming here, along with the sunflowers and daffodils. On the windowsill, carnations sit dipped in food coloring. The children are learning about plant biology by watching the flowers turn blue as their roots sip the painted water, drawing it up into their outstretched leafiness.

Each child gets to pick a symbol, which is used to identify each other in writing before they can manipulate pencils to form letters on paper or form letters into words in the brain. There is a loft, with wide, climbable steps, filled with soft things and books and a doll or two for reading stories to, should such an inspiration arise. On the main level is a library/yoga room nearly like an octagon and perfect for sitting in circular formations.

As Erin and I chat, it feels like it is an uncanny case of instant recognition. She knew she liked me from the moment she heard my voicemail. I knew I liked her the instant I looked at her Web page. Here in person, the suspicion of a wonderful fit is confirmed in a celebration of spirit, philosophy, and the irrefutable evidence of happy kids who seem to have become part of the classroom in less than 5 minutes.

Chilling outside in the garden, Erin tells me about why she wanted to start her own school rather than work in a daycare or a larger school. "There's no such thing as bad children," says Erin, and she means it. Erin continues, "It's just a matter of figuring out what each kid needs. We need different personalities! I wanted to create a place that's small enough for the kids to be who they are and get what they need to thrive instead of having to fit them into a mold."

Just behind the sunflowers, almost hidden in the shade of a friendly tree, is a little kitchen constructed from old stumps, where someone is making acorn soup. A few feet away, grapes are growing on a meandering vine, entwining itself over a little archway.

Erin infuses the whole vibe of the school with her presence as if she were a preschool fairy with sleeves rolled up to work in the earth. From one teacher's imagination, with the help of a devoted husband, a place has literally come to life where each child's unique imprint is cultivated, yet somehow all the t's are crossed and the i's are dotted in full acquiescence to the powers that certify preschools.

I fill out the paperwork, thankful that our condo in Jersey just sold. The amount we were paying for our mortgage is exactly the amount we will soon be spending on preschool. We say our good-byes and head out, tired and satisfied and happy.

Upon arriving home, I set out a spread of nut butter and hemp-seed butter, apples, tortillas, and semi-frozen blueberries. When we are done with our makeshift, yet enjoyable lunch, I throw a change of clothes for Avriana into a Trader Joe's bag, along with a couple of books, and usher the little ones downstairs to the babysitter, who is here to take out the kiddos while I have a phone appointment with a coaching client.

Once each head has been sufficiently kissed, I head upstairs to find my own center, and in so doing, open up a space for my upcoming client. What I love about coaching is that I don't have to do anything other than what is called for in the moment, and while that may be true of life in general, it is much easier to practice during a one-hour segment with a client, where my work consists of following intuitive leads, offering some inquiries and playful challenges, holding up a mirror, and opening up fresh possibilities. Participating in a coaching session is often exhilarating, as well as liberating. It's exhilarating because I witness the power of people to transform their outlooks and leap into lives that align with who they are created to be, which is how I define ultimate success. At the same time, coaching is liberating because I am very intentionally not in control, not responsible, and totally freed up to offer the floor to the client, who is very intentionally in control and responsible, determining the focus of each session, deciding what success looks like, and how it will be measured, searching his or her own truth-o-meter in response to inquiries, and choosing courageous actions that function like bridges and bungee cords, carrying clients from here to where they want to be, and often turning their self-understanding, and sometimes their lives, upside down in the process. I am with the client and for the client, but that is where my job ends. Only the client can leap, yet she knows she will not fall or fly alone, because my support is solidly unconditional. As her coach, I get to share in the thrill.

After today's session is over, I prep for tomorrow's work, then close my laptop and open my arms wide as the kids I love most in the world come bounding through the door and pile on top of me with a million things out of their mouths all at once. A little fist is exploring my intestinal region and my lips are being squished into an infinity symbol.

12

Other Peoples' Lives

September 23rd, 2009

It's early a.m. I'm in a coffee shop preparing to do my first corporate coaching with an employee and an employer in the same room. I'm scribbling notes in a coffee shop when I get the cancellation email. That's okay. She's still covering my childcare expenses, so I can work on other stuff, no extra cost outlay. "No extra cost outlay" is one of my husband's favorite phrases, and I have been incorporating it lately. I file for a Trademark of Lifeshop, my little conceptual merger of life coaching in a playful workshop-style format. I'm thinking a store with apparel and fun lifestyle products eventually. My first Lifeshop event is tonight. I have a pretty good outline, centered on the theme, "The One Thing: Clarifying and Committing to One Life-Changing Action," but I'm still tweaking some things based on the feel I get from the host about who will be there and why. I look at my computer screen and see that it's 12:02. Time's up. I close my folder of scribbled ideas and hop in the car to pick up the kids.

The afternoon with the kids progresses about as you'd expect it to when the mom in question is preoccupied with wrapping up prep for an important work project while trying to arbitrate sibling squabbles and dole out snacks.

"Yes Avriana, you had the train first. I hear that. I understand Gabe. You really want the train and it's taking too long for her to give you a turn. I'm sure two peacemakers like the two of you can find a way to work it out."

"Nika, I hear that you're hungry. You are fully capable of getting yourself a snack."

"Just a minute, Avsi, I'll be right there to help you wipe your bum."

"Yeah, Gabe, look at that circle. It looks like you're really focusing and having fun with your drawing."

In between trying to rehearse my introduction to the evening's event and design a format for collaborative ground rules to be created by the group, I keep turning the front burner on and off for tea, perpetually pouring myself hot water for self-soothing.

I met Linda, the host of the impending Lifeshop, on the deck of BridgePort Brewery, a few weeks after we moved downtown. Linda probably said something about how cute the kids were, and I probably smiled and said something nice about her necklace, and we got talking. Linda turned out to be a fellow transplant, and she reassured us that she understood everything we were going through, although I wasn't quite sure what she was referring to, specifically. Then she bought my kids a stack of cookies that lasted us a week. I found out later she was drunk that first time we met, but when I sent her off with a business card and an offer to do a Lifeshop for her and her friends, I just thought she was friendly. After all, West Coasters are notoriously friendlier than East Coasters, and I didn't have a very long history from which to gage how friendly is the friendly that happens after two or three beers.

Well, lo and behold, a few weeks later, Linda said she found my business card and wanted a refresher on what I was offering. She thought the Lifeshop sounded like a cool idea, so we set something up. Which is how I came to be expected on the Fifth Floor of Irving Lofts at 6:30 this evening. As I pour my eighth cup of hot water over a limp, used-up tea bag, I make a note to myself: Prepare further in advance in order to have the option to be fully present with the kids, without feeling utterly unprepared for a job.

When the sitter arrives, I confess my nervousness as I squeeze into black heels I wouldn't ordinarily walk in for more than a block.

"It'll be fine. It'll be great," says my ever sweet and encouraging sitter.

"Thanks. I hope so!"

I place all my stuff into a Trader Joe's bag: poster board, pens, skinny pieces of blank paper that I cut earlier, letter-size blank paper, a glue stick, rack cards, business cards, and a jar of mostly eaten hemp spread to spoon-feed myself at the park before heading by foot over to my host's condo, which is a few streets up, then over two blocks.

I knock on the door and it is opened into a spacious home glinting with huge granite-top counters and stainless-steel appliances. A small group of thirtyish to fortyish women are seated at a table sipping wine and immersed in gossip.

As the evening unfolds, augmented by a gourmet platter of grapes, cheeses partnered with perfect cheese knives, pinot noir, slices of prosciutto, water crackers, and sugary cakes, what strikes me most about this intimate group of six high-powered professional women is their virtual starvation for profound connection. I lead and facilitate and offer a space; they seem happy to in some sense ignore me and gnaw into the important places of their lives, where their souls live in near-isolation. One woman confesses that she's in a bad marriage, but isn't ready to leave. Not yet, anyway. In the meantime, she dreams of traveling to South America and enjoying whorish, liberated things.

A blonde woman in her early thirties confesses, for the first time to most of these friends, that she is getting a divorce because her husband cares more about getting ahead in his career than about her and he isn't interested in changing his priorities. Tears fill this woman's eyes as she says she's fine and screw him if he doesn't want to work it out. In addition to heartbreak over the end of a marriage she thought was forever, she is really upset at having to rent an apartment. "I try to say that having granite countertops doesn't matter, but it kind of does." The other women nod in agreement. "Yeah, it does," they echo back in harmony. "Isn't it a step backwards, instead of forwards?" "It's only temporary," one friend consoles.

A middle-age woman in a stylish dress has a different perspective. Having achieved every form of professional accolade, she hasn't yet been successful in relationships. Still, she is clear on one thing: Nicer stuff doesn't make you happier. Once married, she remembers when they lived in a small house in a friendly neighborhood filled with backyard cookouts and kids playing outdoors. "That's when we were happiest. Then we upgraded to the bigger house in the executive neighborhood and we weren't happy."

As the stories tumble out, common themes, yet unique individuals, emerge, as the gathered circle confesses wild fantasies, insecurities, and intimate life situations, all the while considering the inquiry, "What is one thing you haven't done that you want to do before you die?" As the last activity winds down, with each woman placing an action she commits to, along with a date she will do it by, on a shared poster that will be gifted to the host, there is an intimate feeling in the room. The evening's "Motto of the Evening" emerges from the lips of a brunette who works as a recruiter: YDB. You Deserve Better. As if passing around a talking stick, each woman, without cue, echoes the phrase, and then, one by one, the guests disperse to their own lives.

I take the elevator to the ground level and out into the night, tired, fulfilled, and longing for sleep. I walk home on the lonely, quiet streets, with only the occasional pedestrian or car. Heels clicking on the sidewalk, this is one of those times I'm glad I live in the Pearl. I can't help wondering if the women I just gathered with would judge me if they knew that I live in—oh, no, heaven forbid—gasp—an apartment—and an affordable-housing unit, at that. I can't help but laugh at the fittingness of living in partially subsidized housing in the most expensive neighborhood in Oregon, what with my dad being the son of parents who slaved over chicken coops to scrimp and save enough to send him to college, while my mom is the descendent of people who came over on the *Mayflower*, owned a plantation, and developed and patented Vick's VapoRub.

I swipe my FOB and the main door of my building clicks open. I walk up the now-quiet stairs and down the hall to my apartment, which I find unlocked. Inside the only sound is the whirring of the dishwasher. I brush my teeth, drink some water, and crawl into our outstretched futon, wrapping my arms fully around my husband who is 85 percent asleep. Draping my left leg instinctively over his warm, cozy body, I smile a prayer of thanks for the yumminess of his physicality, which houses within it my soul mate.

Things have not always been easy or perfect. When we lived in Jersey, I once moved into the windowless room in the loft for a few weeks to try to find my own pulse, that inner sense of self that

I could no longer palpate in the bottomless ocean of isolation that flows from the confluence of unmet expectations and helplessness and fear. I experienced that confluence over and over during my husband's med school years, and I wondered if I'd ever find my way home to the guy I fell in love with. It turns out he felt the same way; it's just that at the time he wasn't exactly conscious of feeling it.

When I said I hated the entire medical training infrastructure, and that when I agreed to come with him on this trip, I didn't bargain for *this,* he took it personally. He heard, "I don't support you." When I railed against the arbitrariness of schedules and how an 80-hour work week during residency didn't fit with my idea of equal parenting or a healthy, flowing family life, he couldn't grasp why I wasn't thrilled that it was no longer the 120-hour work week that residency was a few years ago. He was the idealist: "Of course we can make this work and be happy." I was the realist—or the cynic, depending on your perspective: "What the fuck? How can you say that when I'm the one who will have to endure the sacrifice of the life I envision for us?" He thought I knew more or less what I was getting myself into when I jumped off love's cliff. I had no idea until it was too late. A little like choosing a natural childbirth and knowing it will be hard but not knowing that it will be excruciating and long and that the contractions will come so close you'll still be shaking even when you get to rest for 2 whole minutes or less. Unfortunately, they don't offer epidurals for wives of medical students or interns. There is a name for people who use needles to block out long-term pain: addicts.

But then, looking back, maybe I was addicted to the drama ... or to the pain.

Every time we tried to work out "our issues," it was like those little thumb traps where the harder you tug, the tighter it gets. We misunderstood each other 12 times in 10 minutes over idiotic things, and parsing apart the communication crash did little to bring any true sense of intimacy. He didn't think anything was deeply wrong. While I saw a deadening wall rising up between us, all he saw was part of "the seasons of life." I think we were both right, because eventually each grew up enough to finally listen to each other with an open heart. We started to discover from lived experience that the roles we act out—the ones we most fiercely defend, because we think they define "who we are"—often turn out to be inherited identities cloaking the place inside where our unfettered free self can choose who we want to be in the story of our lives. And a shift occurred. We made choices to water the seeds of healing. Healing is a often a process, but somewhere along the path, it shifts from dressing wounds to growing and opening up and letting light in, and when that shift happens, you find that you're in it together and that even healing ghosts from the past can be fun and liberating.

I was finally able to see that I did choose this and that while, in retrospect, I probably would have benefited from taking more time on my own after the ending of my first marriage to find my footing and feel independent, I would choose to leap off love's cliff with my current husband even if I could go back and make the choice again. I also saw that because my love is truly called to be a physician—it's in his fingers and in his eyes and his everything—I could not love him and undermine his dream.

And if being true to me meant loving him and letting him be who he is, whatever trail that leads us down, I figured there must be a way to be true to the other parts of who I am as well, *even* without the help of the entire medical training infrastructure.

It's funny. When I chose to own the key to my own happiness and to stop blaming my misery on things outside myself having to do with my husband, I got the love of my life back, as if handed to me from behind the veil of mystery. I don't know how that all works, but I'm happy it does. I think of this as I squirm into a comfy position and kiss my love's neck. He snuggles into me too and a smile like mine creeps across his face.

13

Imagination, Inadvertent Killing, and the Person in the Wall

September 26th, 2009

Imaginative play is officially in. Research is confirming intuitive common sense. Consequently, free play, creativity, and spontaneous inventiveness are now being labeled as valuable, as if we parents need an outward stamp of approval to justify allowing our kids to unfold naturally. Instead of worrying over whether our kids can print their names by age three, we now have permission to view the expression of imaginative capacities as precocious, as well as precious, which is great, since I used to guilt-trip myself for not doing enough "educational" activities with my kids.

Today Avriana used a small clump of green clay to create a boat, and then a bed, complete with pillow and covers so that "a girl can sleep there." Then she made her cheese snack into Steve from *Blue's Clues.* Gabe made his jelly brown-rice bread sandwich into a "cracker bus," and used small pieces of tortilla to make Steve and some kids. I was so proud. I was most proud of actually paying attention, tuning in, being with them, and their capacity to imagine. I felt relief to let the kids be who they are, instead of feeling like I ought to be printing out daily letter sheets and designing structured educational activities for every block of time.

Of course, Gabe likes worksheets. I don't have to plan them or print them out. He'll take the initiative himself. He'll sit there with a workbook, tracing letters, circling numbers, with the utmost contentment. "Can you write me some more math problems, Mom?" I make four circles, a plus sign, and three circles. He counts each group and then adds them up altogether.

"Seven!" Gabe's four-year-old face lights up to a million watts.

I wonder how each child's early predilections will express themselves later in life. It takes all kinds, truly it does. Gabe chews on a piece of cheese while he works. He isn't as good at chewing as he is at math. Just as he is informing me gleefully that 8 plus 8 is 16, out of his mouth falls a slobbery, clumpy ball of cheese. It drops on his paper, and he laughs. "Mommy, there's cheese on my paper!"

Last night my husband and I double-dated with some friends. The girl, Connie, is one of our old babysitters who just transitioned to a full-time job as psych counselor. Once in a while, she still hangs out with the kids in exchange for money on the weekends, but mostly these days we are friends. Connie's boyfriend, Kevin, is an ER doc.

"How's work in the Emergency Department?" my husband inquires.

"I didn't kill anyone this week," Kevin answers.

"That's more than I can say," responds my husband, shaking his head.

My love is referring to a woman who had surgery, then died a few days later from a stroke. It was my love who dosed and prescribed the anticoagulant she was given prior to surgery. Give too much of this sort of medicine and the patient risks bleeding out; give too little and you risk clots, leading to stroke, like what ended up happening. The patient whose earthly life ended from an oxygen-deprived brain was a sweet old lady who my husband really liked.

I try to reassure my love that even if it could have been his fault, a kind old lady like that would probably be very understanding from the other side. "Maybe unconsciously she was ready to go and volunteered to participate in your learning experience in this way ..." I put out there as a possibility.

Kevin shares his strategy for how to cope when a patient dies on your watch: "That's when you say, 'Nobody died who wasn't supposed to die'."

Nervous laughter settles and eventually conversation moves to talk of balloon festivals in New Mexico, sibling relationships, ideas about raising teenagers, and giving people the benefit of the doubt even if they're literally crazy.

As we dip our last pita slices in hummus, Connie tells a story of something that happened on a psych ward once. An inpatient heard banging and screaming coming from the wall and told the staff. Of course, no one believed him at first, because of his insanity. Later they discovered another patient had tried to escape and somehow got stuck in the wall. Thankfully, the escapee survived, and a lesson learned: Even crazy people often have something important tell us, if we are open to hearing the unexpected. Conversely, lots of time normal people listen to other normal people saying things that aren't important in the least.

When the bill comes, Kevin wants to pay for all of us.

"After all, I'm the Attending."

"Well, next time it's our treat," I say, "because technically I'm *her* employer."

14

Failing

September 28th, 2009

I failed. A score of 80 percent was needed to pass. I got 79 percent. I'm talking about the written driver's exam for the state of Oregon. Either the Oregon version is harder than the Massachusetts one or I have lost a critical amount of brain cells from parenting insomniac children. Or maybe I was just too cavalier.

When I took the written test as a teenager, I studied hard, knowing I can't easily memorize random facts that have little bearing on life. I can't convince my hippocampus that certain bundles of facts are important if I can't find the relevance. For example, there was a question on the test about whether you have to take the chains off by March 1st, March 15th, or April 15th. I don't ever use chains on my tires, so why would I think to make a note of when you have to remove them?

This time around, I glanced at the Driver's Manual the night before the test for a few minutes, but it was late by the time we got home from hanging out with Connie and Kevin, and I didn't feel like pulling an all-nighter, so I went to bed. After all, I'm not in high school or college, why should I have to stay up late and study for a lame test?

After dropping the kiddos off at school, I studied for an hour at a coffee shop off of Interstate Ave for an hour before the test. I committed to memory the 0.08 percent alcohol thing. I knew my right- and left-hand signals, and that parking uphill you turn your wheels out, whereas parking downhill you turn the wheels in. I figured, after driving for over a decade, the rest ought to be common sense. Somehow none of what I studied appeared on the test, and a whole bunch of random stuff, like the thing about the precise date for tire chain removal, showed up instead. I panicked and started rushing through, hoping to somehow just make it get over faster and hoping for the best. The computer screen informs me that hoping for the best is not an effective test-taking strategy by flashing my results: "You failed."

On the way home, I think, *idiot*. Tears stream down my face, and I lick the salty wetness and groan. I try to think positive thoughts: You're only an idiot about some things. You have strengths too!

Meanwhile, I forget to look at the signal light on my way home and somebody honks at me. People never honk in Portland. I do make it home without crashing into any pedestrians.

Failing the written exam on technicalities reminds me of how I once got points off on a spelling test after getting all the words correct. My error? I forgot to write the "a" at the end of my own name! In college I did the same thing: Following the completion of a well-written research paper, I forgot to put my name on the cover sheet. Points off.

I try to delegate out my areas of weakness so I'm free to live from my strengths. Unfortunately, the DMV Website specifically says it's illegal to delegate the written driver's exam to another person. What's up with that?

When Nika asks me how my test went, I tell her that I failed, but that I will keep trying until I pass. What I really want to do is sell my car and never drive again, but for the sake of being a good example, I won't. My daughter looks at me with genuine empathy. I remind her and myself in the process that the important thing is to learn from failures or mistakes, and then try again, understanding that greatness is not the result of instant success, but of unstoppable perseverance. I mention Edison and the light bulb and how he interpreted his unsuccessful attempts at inventing the light bulb not as failure but as finding 8001 ways that don't work. I just hope I don't have to take the written driver's test 8001 times before I figure it out.

I'll be at the DMV again on Tuesday.

15

The Glass Elevator

September 29th, 2009

Nika's other dad is in town to spend time with her, so today our Saturday family outing is short one member. Usually the missing person is a mid-thirties male, instead of a seven-year-old girl. It's odd having Nika off on her own adventure apart from us, but we find a subtly different rhythm and enjoy the day.

My love and I take the little ones out for an adventure on the Max train. I lean into my husband and he consoles me over yesterday's failure. I don't feel any less stupid, but I do feel unconditionally loved. Gabe and Avsi don't seem to hold me in any less regard for my failure either.

At first the four of us try to find an eco-friendly festival that is supposedly a brief walk from a certain Max stop, but turns out to be a long distance away. We give up on that plan and notice that we are in the vicinity of Gabe and Avsi's new preschool, where they will be starting this coming Tuesday. I'm elated to get to show it off to my love, even if only from the outside. We picnic on a grassy area near the sidewalk, nibbling on pancakes, walnuts, cranberries, and cheese. The sun is shining and it feels good to relax together. I hope Nika is having fun. I'm pretty confident she is enjoying her time as much as we are, and that thought fills me with happiness. I'm aware of a contented longing for her.

On the way home, I spy a glass elevator over by the Amtrak station. Gabe has a thing for glass elevators. I like them too. They remind me of *Charlie and the Chocolate Factory*. The four of us run like the wind toward the glass elevator, as if chasing a treasure. I love that feeling of wonder, of letting life be magical, of leaping or galloping instead of walking respectably.

As the glass elevator rises with the four of us in it, our perspective shifts. We see the insides of potted flowers, instead of the outsides, the tops of people's heads, and the ant-like patters they make walking around to and fro. Gabe and Avsi hop out of the elevator, followed by their parents. Outside the elevator, there is a walking bridge, from which we can peer at the rooftops of trains. A daring person could easily jump from bridge to train, probably without incident.

The four of us ride the glass elevator down nice and easy and set out for home, my love and I each carrying an increasingly heavy kid. We cross the Broadway Bridge by foot, turn down our street, climb the stairs, unlock the door, and utterly fatigued, collapse for a few minutes of happy sprawled-out rest.

In the evening, a sitter comes for an hour and a half. Living in the city, that is plenty of time for a date.

My love and I stroll unhurriedly toward Living Room Theaters, which is one block up from Powell's Books. I sit in my love's lap comfortably, and we flirt over a glass of wine, a sandwich, and a hot chocolate served in a flute glass. I still feel tired, but underneath the tired feeling is a surge of happiness. The old heaviness that traveled with us through medical school has been replaced by a joyful intimacy, gained from a life being fully lived, individually and together. We laugh and talk freely, caressing each other's hands, while exchanging friendly conversation with our wonderful server, who goes by Christina, instead of "Chrrristina Marie" (with the rolled Spanish r) because, she explains, her dad's white, and she feels like, "C'mon, I'm too white to be Chrrristina Marie." We tell her about our three kids and she tells us about her future: "I'm Mexican and my boyfriend is Spanish, so I know we're going to have like 20 kids. That's why I'm waiting at least 10 years!"

Lingering over the last sips of hot chocolate and wine, a thought comes over me that it's important to embrace this free, happy feeling and let it soak into my essential core. Even on less floaty fun days, I want to remember that this is who we are. My love and I walk home, arm in arm, skipping here and there. On the way home, we scheme about a weekend getaway for two when my mom comes to visit in October. I comment that I can't believe we actually have the energy to get excited about going somewhere cool. It's been a long time since I had enough energy to think beyond the thing in front of me.

In the unfolding blanket of evening, we savor each other's intimate presence in the way a man and woman in love do best.

16

Sabbath, My Ass

October 1st, 2009

S unday is here and instead of a lovely, slothful Sabbath, it's back to reality. I know, I know, it's all reality—the perfect moments like last night, and the imperfect ones like when the oatmeal is caked over every inch of your countertop and all three kids are fighting, fussing, or needing something all before you've had the chance to stretch, yawn, and say "Good morning" to the dawning light, which is how things are going so far today. I have heard that life is literally what you make it, that reality is little more than infinite potential obliging us by taking on specific forms based on our intentions, expectations, and observations. Add to that the fact that human beings have an incessant need to interpret what we observe, and you have a lot of subjectivity built into life itself. If I change my intentions and expectations and then I watch what happens, well, theoretically, I can shift the fabric of what's truly happening, like a chain reaction. What a fun idea, for when you're having a good day.

What a bunch of bull when you're the only adult in the middle of a whining, biting tantrum, while your partner is off at a weekend event for his career. My husband is spending his Sunday at a regional training on advanced postpartum care, and I wonder what good advanced postpartum care is, if it doesn't extend through how to support, and as they say "manage," maternal health through early childhood. To be honest, my health could use some improvement. According to my naturopath, my adrenals are depleted and my hormones are whacko, and I have a syndrome that makes me prone to acne and ovarian cysts. It is likely I built up these issues from years of cumulative damage, along with genetic predispositions. I'm thinking about how it's Sunday and my love *shouldn't* be away today. He's not even on-call. Why couldn't they have given him a day off from clinic to get the extra training? But *noooo,* then they might lose some of the money they make off of him. And even though he had nothing to do with scheduling the dang training, I blame him, thoroughly. It's his fault that he *chose* to go into this field. He's not here and I need him. "It's your fault" is the phrase I can't get out of my mind. I seethe at him from a distance. Last night's dreaminess has turned into a daytime nightmare. Sure the kids are throwing blocks at each other's heads, but mostly the nightmare is one I'm playing inside my own noggin, as I count the minutes until my love (who at the moment I really don't like) walks in the door and I get to take a walk, read a few pages of a book, and have an opportunity to take a few breaths to calm my sizzling nerves. I'm expecting him at 5:30. That's when he said he'd be home, and I'm watching the clock, checking every increment of time until my expectation is fulfilled.

I get a call around noontime. The voice on the line is hemming and hawing, saying he loves me and ... and ... well, so, um, it turns out the faculty has specially ordered cow tongues, on which they're expecting the interns to practice perineal repair until 6:30.

"Fuck."

I say it loudly, over the phone, in front of the kids. If the program had the decency or organizational agility to put things like "special cow tongue activity until 6:30" on the interns' schedule, I could adapt myself to it. What is wrong with these people? Why

51

add Chinese water torture to the list of ways residency challenges family life?

Gabe and Avsi are staring at me, wondering about the word I just said. "Mommy said a bad word. Try not to say it." Nika is in her room ensconced in a fort of blankets, books, and other items of interest. With a tiny bit of luck, my bad word missed her lovely ears.

In spite of the blow, the evening unfolds with peaceful interactions washing over the kids and me, like a calming grace. It's when you curse if you have to, and then, when you truly know you've lost the fight, you give up and decide to be open to happiness outside the circumstances of your choosing that life smiles at your surrender and offers you treasures you didn't think to ask for until they are in your hands.

In my hands is a knife and I use it to slice strawberries for a picnic. There is something in the lusciousness of the strawberries that awakens in me a whimsical longing to offer something beautiful up out of this day.

Upon finding that we have no protein in the house, I take the kids out to Lil' Green Grocer to pick up turkey to enfold in our corn tortillas. Once our supper is packed in a Trader Joe's bag and slung over my shoulder, the kids negotiate their scooters out of our little entryway and down the hall without a collision. Each of them can now carry their own scooter down the steps to our building's lobby. I usher them safely across streets and train tracks until we get to the beginning of the Greenway path, which runs along the Willamette River. Avsi glides along in a sleeveless mint-green dress. Gabe is wearing his blue and neon-green winter coat, weaving like a laid-back slalom skier. Nika cruises, as cool as a cucumber, in her comfiest ripped jeans, covered in doodles.

We plop down on a bench with unusual tranquility. Watching the sun glow low on the horizon, the rippling, flowing water has a soothing effect. Food is chomped and shared peaceably, without event. Legs dangle from the bench, swinging softly. Avsi smiles up at me. Nika and I talk about our favorite part of our favorite book, *The Penderwicks*. Gabe coos softly, singing on the breeze. How can such a polluted river be so healing? Fatigue melts into mellow gratitude and quiet enjoyment of the treasures by my sides.

I send out a prayer of thanks for the Willamette, and a wish for its cleansing.

17

Toy Bins and Cow Tongues

October 1st/2nd, 2009

Later, at home, with the sun almost gone, Avriana has at last settled on which toothbrush to use and Gabe has shown me what he can add on his calculator and both have been tucked in with stories. Nika helps me clean up. It's the first time I have seen her take initiative in this area. I'm stunned and happy, and I don't quite know how to react. The last thing I want to do is jinks it, so I try to just flow with it, blinking my eyes twice to double-check that my oldest daughter actually said, "Mom, let's clean."

Nika's idea is to sort through our toy bins. With her effort, the toy bins transform into *feng-shui* holders of toys. Then I notice that all the tiny toys have been arranged on display in the living-room window: action figures, trinkets, doll beds, all lined up as if our Toy Story were being filmed in our living room, which is also the adult bedroom where the futon rolls out at night. I remember doing the same sort of enchanting thing as a kid, yet my gut is squeezing and my jaw is clenched at the new level of invasion of kid stuff into the last holdouts of adult territory. I try to be gentle explaining to Nika that it is a lovely, creative display, yet I do not want to look at toys covering every inch of the living room, since after the kids fall asleep, it is the only adult space in our home. It must sound rude and exclusive to her. I remember being a kid and totally not getting why adults would not want to have me around simply because of my age. It seemed unfair. I can see the look of disappointment cross Nika's face. "But why, Mama?" I grope for words to explain the urgency I feel for having a little space that is kid-free. In the end, all I can say is "I totally understand why this doesn't make sense to you, and it has something to do with having a time and place where I just get to be a person, and not just someone who takes care of the kids she loves. When you are an adult, it will be awesome to hang out with you late at night, in the grownup space."

Later, my love walks through the door. I'm half nice, half giving the cold shoulder. Eventually niceness wins out. Or maybe it's curiosity that wins out, because I really can't imagine what it must be like to sew up the area on a woman between her vagina and anus using a cow tongue. It's like two gross concepts wrapped into one, and I have to know what it was like.

"Pretty gross," my love says. "It was remarkable how similar the cow tongue is to that, uh, that area of the body on a person." I laugh. It is good to have adult space.

By 11 at night, "adult space" is a concept that doesn't mean anything beyond a hopeful idea. Gabe has climbed into bed and made himself quite at home. He likes to drape his leg over me, just like I do with my love.

Avriana wakes up at 1:30 in the morning. She is screaming uncontrollably. I make out that she wants hemp milk and wants to force her brother out of bed. She insists, tearfully, that "Gabe is a scary boy." Did she have a dream about him whacking her or tugging her hair? A few minutes before dawn breaks, quiet enters in.

An hour or so later, my love stirs and rolls out of bed. I watch him, half-asleep darting around, toothbrush in his mouth, while he puts on scrubs and socks. The toothbrush no longer in his mouth, he comes over to where I'm lying, wondering if it really has to be another day already. I kiss him groggily. When I push myself out of bed a few minutes later, I can tell instantly he is gone. I can feel it, without searching the rooms. Fortunately, he left us with cream of buckwheat cereal still toasty-warm in the pot.

18

License to Be a Freak

October 2, 2009

Today I'm dropping my two little ones off at preschool for the very first time. A friend who knows the kids well is with me. After the big drop-off, our next stop is the DMV for Take Two of my Oregon Driver's License Test. I'm hoping to pass with flying colors. In any event, it is a big day for my little ones and for me.

As soon as we enter the school doors, Gabe and Avsi are off in a heartbeat, free and at home in this new environment, like fish released into a sheltered pond. It is a tingly, fulfilling feeling to see them free and independent, yet protected. Avriana immediately climbs the wooden ladder into the loft area, where she starts reading a book to her "baby." Above her is a rectangular mirror on the ceiling, offering a new perspective, should she want one. Gabe briefly involves himself with a fire truck before gravitating toward the cash register with all those delicious numbers to punch. Gabe is the only child I have ever met who prefers workbooks and calculators to Elmo or kid games or Toy Story. I'm sure there are others like him; I just haven't met them.

I chat with the teacher, Erin. I offer my utter gratitude for who she is and what she does—the way she attends to the little ones, connecting with them where they're at and helping them create a learning plan based on their interests.

I reflect on that phase of life where you can be whatever you want, without limitations: a hero or a mommy, a cash-register operator, or a gourmet chef. You can play using the same tools for different purposes: A broom can be used for cleaning or for flying; a cape can belong to Little Red Riding Hood or Superman. You can paint with whatever color you want, and you can mix your colors in a way that knocks your socks off, and a teacher like Erin isn't going to tell you "you didn't do it right."

Even a lesser preschool teacher than Erin would never tell a kid, "Grow up and get an office job that pays the bills and just try to get through life, because that's all that can be expected." In a school like Erin's, you can help each other build something, or you can do your own thing for a while. You can make choices, as long as you aren't hurting anyone. And even if you hurt someone, you aren't labeled bad. You have the opportunity to have the implications of your actions pointed out: "When you waved that block in the air, it hit Sally in the face. I think she's hurting. What could you do to help her feel better? What's a safer way to play with blocks for next time?"

Imagine a world free of condemnation and full of opportunities for discovery and reconciliation.

I think if there's one thing I do for my coaching clients it's help them get back to that place of innocent wonderment, full of possibility. It's so easy for grownups to seal ourselves up in a box built of "shoulds" when life is full of choices and implications and infinite ways to interact with those implications.

After I have given my little ones kisses and hugs (more for my sake than theirs, apparently), my friend and I head to the DMV, where I spend half an hour sweating and experiencing low-grade hyperventilation.

I finally pass the test, within one point.

Phew. While my papers are getting processed, I chat with the jolly, warm-hearted African guy who works behind the counter at the DMV. Last time I was here, before he knew I had just failed my test, this big African Buddha in an *aloha* shirt asked teasingly, "Can you speak Swahili?" I say in my loudest voice, "Jambo Sana!" When you have just failed your driver's test, it is good to do something joyful and absurd, and I happened to know that "Jambo Sana" means a really big hello. I learned that from a kid CD, one that the children request repeatedly. "Jambo Sana" is the only song I like on that disk.

Today my African friend muses aloud about my New Jersey license plate and asks about where I'm from originally. I tell him I grew up in Massachusetts and he suddenly gets an odd, confused frown from forehead to chin. "I went to Massachusetts once. I was in Boston. If you smile at people and say 'Good Morning!' they look at you like you're crazy. Like they're thinking, what's wrong with you? I went to the gas station to ask for directions, and nobody even helped me. They just look at you like, find it yourself."

I can only nod with total understanding. Every place has its hidden diamonds, if you know where and how to look. I found a few diamonds on the East Coast, but it seemed like people were so tightly wound and private that when I smiled at strangers, operating on the innocent assumption that, by and large, a stranger is nothing other than a friend you haven't met, I got this look like "You are a freak with three heads." Overall, I prefer the more laid-back posture of Portlanders. Even if I actually were a freak with three heads, that'd be okay, because the city's motto is "Keep Portland Weird."

A few miles across the Columbia River, a different kind of city has the opposite motto: "Keep Vancouver Normal." I think the key to life is to have just the right proportions of weird and normal, with those measurements varying with the individual.

In Portland, even though it's cool to be weird, even if you are a three-headed freak, you still need a license to drive, drink, and get into the zoo if you don't have your member card on hand. Maybe that's the normal part of the equation. Thankfully, I can now legally drive my own personal flavor of weirdness from place to place, enjoy an occasional alcoholic beverage, and hang out with other weird creatures, even if I forget my zoo card.

When I pick up Avsi and Gabe from preschool, their round little faces light up with wonder, while in effervescent screeches they tell me about their day. Avsi tells me about how she painted a pink princess and played with Zachi in the loft. Gabe is elated because he showed his friend how to build an oval train track.

A few hours later, Nika gets home from Chapman Elementary School, happy, tired, and ready for quick hugs and then she's off to her room to lose and find herself in a book. Like her mom, Nika prefers real books over contrived homework.

As we chat and snuggle later in the evening, after the kiddos are in bed, she says, "Can I homeschool? School is too easy. It's so boring."

I mentioned how much she likes friends and how, as much as I like playing, I can't do it all day. She has this look of recognition, remembering when we did homeschool for first grade.

When I found out other people's children were peeing themselves because the control-freak teacher couldn't tolerate bathroom breaks during "specials," I took my daughter's sudden onslaught of daily tantrums to heart and yanked her from a Quaker-based school that had been idyllic up to that point.

Homeschooling for first grade was a gift with a high cost. While it clearly brought my oldest daughter and me closer, it was a rocky trip for us both. Our needs were frequently at odds, what with Nika being a six-year-old who craved constant attention, and me being a burnt-out mom with two terrifically terrible and terribly terrific toddlers to care for, in addition to trying to be an educator and playmate for my oldest, all the while nursing plenty of resentments about the arbitrary, unavoidable, and often unpleasant ride of being strapped to a husband in medical school. The ideals I cherished and the demands placed on my shoulders were too much to bear and I broke down often, feeling unable to truly honor the full spectrum of my values, or carry the load of responsibility that fell to me.

I'm open to homeschooling again in the future, when our whole family life shifts to a new place. In fact, I would cherish the chance to learn with my kids if timing, inclination, and destiny line up. For the time being, Nika and I both know deep inside that she needs a crew of classmates to chase around on the playground, along with her new best friend, with whom she plays Pegasus and daily makes a home out of the large leafy tree that sits watch over recess a few feet from the playground.

Nika looks thoughtful. "Well, can we do a little homeschooling together on our own, like maybe Mondays and Thursdays when I get home from school? "

"Absolutely."

"Do you love me Mama? I want to hear you say it."

"Yes Nikasua. If all the seven-year-old girls in the universe were lined up, I would pick you, every time, 100 percent."

"Really?"

"Yep."

19

Crash Course

October 7th, 2009

It's a clear, blue October morning in the Pacific Northwest with crisp, wide-open skies. Everything you could want on an airy fall day.

It seems far too lovely a day to smash a side mirror on the way out of a garage, but I do just that. It's what I get for thinking about the perfection of cool blue skies, instead of focusing on maneuvering out of an itsy-bitsy parking space between an old beat-up Ford and a cement post. I don't use that one anyway, I think to myself. Better to lose the right side mirror than the left, since I'm well trained, thanks to my father, to look over my left shoulder, instead of relying only on glass-reflected images. Apparently I require further training on looking over my left shoulder on crystal-clear October days.

I drop off Nika and her carpool buddy, Lilly, at Chapman Elementary, quickly squeezing my growing daughter who seems too young to already be getting shy about mommy hugs in public. At least she still wants me to do her ponytail in the morning. I watch the girls bound energetically toward their classrooms, pink backpacks bobbing behind them.

When the little ones and I arrive at preschool, minus a side mirror, Erin tells me that the other day Avriana told her classmate, Finnigan, "I love you." And Finnigan replied, "I love you, too, Avriana."

I have a little extra time alone in the house today, since my love is on night float. He will get off work in time to pick up Gabe and Avsi from preschool, then head home for a few short hours before putting on fresh scrubs and driving back to the hospital for another 30 hours of checking medicines, updating charts, answering pages, admitting new patients in the wee hours of a day that hasn't yet come, ordering tests, and talking with family members of critically ill people, people in ICU.

Many interns shun the job of holding family meetings, where the news is uncertain at best, terminal at worst, but this is where my love shines. His compassion is unmanufactured and he is skilled at intuiting what will be most helpful to the families, as well as a natural at translating 14-syllable jargon into basic human language. Discussing advanced directives, such as DNR orders, indicating the patient does not want to be resuscitated if they stop breathing, or their heart stops, and other details about what to do if a patient is crashing are felt by my love to go beyond a legal concern, or even a matter of cold ethics. For my love, these conversations are an opportunity for the family to come together to talk about the person they love, even if they have not talked with each other productively in years. When life and death mingle in the same room, estrangement can give way to intimacy, and my love is an expert at facilitating interpersonal connection and understanding, while acquiring clarity about how invasive, or not, the patient and their family want the medicine team to be should the eventuality of impending death present itself sooner instead of later.

20

Life Is Not a Sprint

October 10th, 2009

I've always clung to the idea that when it comes to life's challenges, I prefer short, intense ones over long endurance tests. My mantra, for as long as I can remember, has been: "I'm a sprinter, not a marathon runner." Unfortunately, parenting is not a sprint, nor is undergoing your husband's medical training, or healing chronic health issues. My naturopath, who is also trained as an MD, says that my bodily imbalances will take two or three years to heal. I'm longing for a quick fix. Dang, where is it?

The Infinite Wisdom of the Universe seems to get high off of trumping our "I'm not" and "I'll never ..." with "Oh yes you are" and "Oh you sure will."

I once swore I'd never move back to New England, where I grew up, unless God dragged me kicking and screaming. One night, a crystal-clear message from my intuition made itself known to me: "It's time to move to the Boston area." Funny, the clarity of the inkling incited a feeling of actually *wanting* to move to the Boston area. Following my intuition, I loaded up a U-haul truck, and with my ex in tow, headed to Acton, Massachusetts. A friend of a friend needed a house sitter, so my ex and I lived lives hanging in the balance with our baby daughter for six months rent-free. Thank goodness rent was free, because those were the days when my checks were bouncing, for reasons I couldn't at the time quite figure out.

It all worked out though, because I met my love in that little town I swore I would never go back to, and that was fine indeed, except that it surprised my love when he fell for me and for my kid, because, in addition to never having been "in love" before, while he had run two marathons and didn't shirk from endurance races of any kind, he had his own "I'll never." It went like this:

"I'll never marry a woman who has been previously married and I certainly won't marry anyone with a child." Well then he met me. And my daughter. Do we plan our own surrender before we incarnate on this planet? If he had been paying attention, my love could have seen it coming. When he was in his mid-twenties and dating the same girl he was still dating out of habit, my husband had a dream. In his dream, there was a little girl less than two with golden curls. She was standing by a window, the curtain blowing in the wind. He knew he was not the biological father, yet felt paternal, like a dad toward this little blonde girl. My love knew that he was with the little girl's mother, though she was in the other room, out of sight.

The other day, our street was closed for the Portland Marathon. I asked my love, "Do you miss running in a marathon? " "I always miss running a marathon," he said with a nostalgically dreamy look, edged with the reality that he probably won't run one anytime soon.

Life is overwhelming when you are an intern. Probably the only way my love would run a marathon is if I said, "I want to run a marathon. Let's train together." The thought of getting my love to do something that gives him such joy half makes me want to train for a marathon. Who knows, someday perhaps I'll do a half marathon. At least we are running the marathon of our lives hand-in-hand.

My love falls asleep for an hour so in the afternoon, and in the meantime Nika arrives home from her day at school. After dumping her pink monkey backpack by the door, Nika asks me to give her some learning assignments. A kid who wants to learn when school is done, how freaking cool is that, I think quietly. I create a worksheet for Nika, asking her to respond to questions about a book she's reading. Then I write up a spelling list, comprised of words I find in a random book off the adult shelf. My seven-year-old is insatiable. She wants further learning assignments. This is a kid who, a year ago, incessantly imagined herself to be a waitress named Carly, who was married to this dufus named Rob, played by a life-size stuffed penguin.

In a few minutes, it will be time for my husband to occupy his role as intern for another night at the hospital. He lovingly takes out the trash, just as our sitter arrives. I watch as my love kisses each of our kids on the soft hair of their heads.

My love and I slip out the door and walk down the hall together, arms wrapped around each other in a moving, sideways hug. We jog over to Tanner Springs for a quick banister ride. We try to slide in a new position. Oops! My love loses balance and suddenly he is hanging by one arm, like an awkward, upside-down monkey. I try to pull him up and we fumble around until he is on his feet. Upright, he updates me on his dermatology appointment earlier in the day. He has to go every six months, since he had a melanoma last year, which was caught, thank God, before it spread.

"So I'm sitting in the waiting room, unshaven and scruffy in my scrubs, since I went straight from the hospital to the appointment. I hear a medical assistant call my name. But it was the oddest thing to hear her address me as doctor, even though I was coming in as a patient."

"And how did that make you feel, Doctor," I tease, tickling his underarm.

"Pretty funny."

"Do you feel like a doctor yet?" I inquire.

"Actually, yeah. Most of the time."

I see a goofy look crawl across his face. A long kiss and I watch him stride toward the garage, his exit point into life as an intern.

Later, when I put Nika to bed, she says with carefree resoluteness, "School is just for friends, but oh well, whatever, maybe I'll learn a thing or two."

21

Room Service for One

October 11th, 2009

Hubby is preparing to leave. During night float, it always seems like he's leaving. Then the next day it feels like he is returning from a trip. Just now he looks up at me while bent over stuffing a few items into his bag on his way out.

Out of the blue, he says, as though suggesting we order Thai takeout, "Why don't you take a retreat Friday evening? Take a train somewhere or stay in a hotel and take some time for yourself."

I don't know if it was the bags under my eyes or the strain in my posture on my way to the fridge to fetch something for someone, or a comment I made recently about the weight of night float equaling on-call night after night on the home front addressing pee accidents, bed shuffling, and 3 a.m. toddler wars over pillow territory. I do know that in every feasible way this one person, this love of my life, puts my well-being first. It's who he is.

I roll over the idea in my head.

"I committed to take the kids to Isobel's Clubhouse Family Movie Night. Would you be up for taking them? "

"What time is it?"

"Six-thirty."

"Sounds good."

On Friday afternoon, an hour before I'm due to head out, I have a chance to hop on Priceline. Ask for what you want, I tell myself as I type in my bid: $40 for a 3-star hotel. I don't care where, as long as it isn't at the airport.

I watch William Shatner looking really silly on my computer screen, while an icon spins, telling me that Priceline is negotiating on my behalf.

I get it! In fact, I get upgraded to a 3 1/2–star hotel in Lake Oswego!

In a hurry I throw a few clothes, my makeup bag, a book, a journal, and some floss in a bag and off I go.

Upon entering my room, I set my bag down beside the bed. It's a ritual I have, almost a rule, when it comes to making myself comfortable at a hotel. First I jump on the bed. I adore hotels for the lovely piles of fluffy pillows and the newly cleaned feel of the decor. But above all I love hotels for the bouncy beds and the unfettered freedom to jump myself silly on them. It doesn't matter that I'm the only one here in this hotel room. I leap and bounce till it feels great to collapse into the fluffy pillows and simply be. I take off my shoes, and lying down doing nothing, I breathe. It takes a while to feel that breath easing itself into the peaceful contentment of having nothing to do and nowhere to go.

With evening descending, I order room service, which is delivered in timely, professional, totally fabulous fashion. The woman who comes to my room asks brightly where I'd like the tray. I motion to the coffee table and smile back. "We'll start there." I'm picturing eventually moving the tray onto the bed, but the table seems a fitting place to set it for now. What makes this room service experience perfect is that the person who offered the service seems immensely pleased herself, like she knows how incredibly awesome it is that she has the power to make someone's day simply by showing up with a silver platter.

I take slow, sumptuous bites of a triple cheese chicken quesadilla, soaking in the quiet open space, the utter absence of people making demands on me. I even have a break from having to care for my own needs, thanks to room service. Oh what ecstatic happiness! I chew another mouthful of quesadilla draped in guacamole.

When I'm finished with the platter of supper, I open the door, prop it with my foot, and scoot the tray into the hall. Only I scoot a little too far and my foot loses its holding on the door, which swings resolutely shut. My key is sitting on the desk inside the room, next to the phone. I'm in my pajamas, barefoot, and unquestionably locked out.

I traipse downstairs to the lobby in my PJs and naked feet. It's a little embarrassing, but also a little liberating. I explain my situation at the front desk and am handed another key, no questions asked. "Your other keys will still work," says the concierge with a poker face. I guess physicians aren't the only ones trained to maintain a neutral reaction in the face of other people's unconventional behavior.

That's yet one more thing I love about elegant hotels—they treat you with unqualified classiness. A 2-star hotel would probably have me call my husband who would have to confirm my identity or give a credit card number or something. I once stayed at a 2

1/2–star hotel where the coffeepot had used coffee still in it, and maintenance people hammered on my wall all afternoon and half the night. When I asked how they would like to make it right, the lady at the front desk said, "Well you did pay with Priceline. I really can't give you any further discount than that." On the other hand, at really nice hotels, the best is formally assumed of you, even when you paid $40 on Priceline.

Back in my room, with night forming a velvet blanket around Lake Oswego, I take out a book from my bag and engross myself in it. I sit and do nothing some more. Having time away helps foster perspective on my career and my thoughts and feelings as well as how I interact with my love and my kids. It's funny how I can hear the song of all our hearts so much more clearly with a little space. Oh the lovely songs emanating from each of our souls, contained in these bodies and minds with so many daily collisions of wants and felt needs and knee-jerk reactions. It is easy for the sound of our soul songs to get lost in a sea of everybody's demands, screeching in my ears at a pitch that grates like cat nails on a chalkboard.

After jotting down some notes to myself in my journal, I wonder what to do next with this precious open time where I have full permission to do what I feel like doing. Exhaustion is present in me, but I'm also a little hyper. The freedom to feel my own pulse and whim makes me feel like a kid again.

I turn on the radio and dance from bed to floor and back again, free as a whistling bird. I'm so thankful for the movement of feet and the flinging of arms, the bounce of the lift-ups and the soft pillows that cushion me when I land. I'm thankful too for my love back at home. I wonder what everyone is doing. I know I'll have plenty of time to find out.

When the dance in me is spent, I move toward stillness. It's time to open, to be fully here. Time to pray. My prayers are intermittently interrupted by an inner debate over whether or not to purchase an overpriced pay-per-view chick flick that I'd totally love to watch. Usually I'd say forget it. It's overpriced—what a rip-off. Tonight, I think, I get to do what I want and enjoy it with zero to minimal guilt. With the press of one button, $14.99 is added to my bill and the film starts. "Film" is probably overstating, but the movie is exactly what I need: funny. It's completely predictable and laugh-out-loud hilarious.

In the room next door, I hear a family. A baby wails or laughs from time to time and a toddler talks about trucks. I think about how wonderful kids are. I'm happy. I'm happy here, for this time free of having to do for others, yet opening my tank and letting it fill up with lusciousness and love to offer when I open the door of Apartment 209 tomorrow.

22

Love, Epocrates, and a Pink Flying Saucer

October 12th, 2009

It's a cool evening of simple pleasures. When the babysitter arrives, I stride out in the open air and inhale its freshness, like an oxygen bath that cleans off whatever residue is clinging to me from the day.

I head over to the Urban Grind, and when I get there, my love is sitting at a table for two, looking handsome in his lavender shirt and silvery tie. He is checking email and looking up medical things on his iPhone. I heard a statistic that 93 percent of adults in America own a cell phone. If it's true, I'm one of the 7 percent who doesn't own one. It's sort of mysterious watching other people punching thoughtfully into the little gadgets. You never know if they are looking up the weather or checking out naked pictures or toying around with an app. My love's favorite app is Epocrates. He can look up any medicine, in any dose, and learn any number of things about it: its chemical components, contraindications for giving it, and even what the pill looks like. He can look up how to treat a particular illness, including the evidence for each possible treatment. No longer does a physician need to house every iota of information in their heads, lest they have to pull a 10-pound tome off the shelf and thumb through endless indexes and pages as thin as baklava wrapping. If only med schools would catch up with the times and instead of making students drink from a fire hose of knowledge to memorize and regurgitate on command focus more on fostering the ability to think correctly about medicine. What questions will lead to the best diagnoses? Which treatment plan best matches what the patient wants out of life, given their situation? What style of communication, cultural factors, and accountability can be harnessed to help the patient follow through with lifestyle changes and prioritize taking the medicines prescribed to them? Which medicines can be eliminated or tapered to a lower dose? What does nature have to offer this person, either preventative or as a part of an integrated approach to addressing a health concern? The potential to be freed up from the old need to memorize everything and to focus on learning to think in ways that treat the patient holistically is one possible benefit of the iPhone, along with its undeniable convenience.

I walk toward my love, immersed in his informational world, and as if he can sense me, his gaze looks up and his eyes meet mine with happy recognition. He clicks out of Epocrates, puts his phone away, and stands up to hold me close and kiss me. We are just shy of a make-out session. Time to order. We get a vanilla steamer and a hot chocolate, both to share. An empty couch invites us toward it and we plop into its squishy comfort. We talk and laugh. Everything is funny, as though we are buzzed, only much more wonderful. Our drinks are entirely virgin. We are high on each other alone. It's just one of those whimsical wonderful times when two people's electrons are calibrated for synergistic hilarity and the joy of two who are also one.

When our time is up, I watch my love walk toward his car, hop in, and pull onto the road that will take him into his other world. I walk home, pacing each step for full enjoyment of the evening. The little two are tucked in when I get inside our apartment and Nika is waiting up for me. I feel like some tea and I offer some to my growing girl. "Sure" she says, delighted to be included in an adult ritual.

We sip our strawberry tea together happily, and Nika introduces me to a tiny, furry, plastic little friend named Cuddles, on loan from her friend Lilly. I am then given the grand tour of the little world my daughter has created for Cuddles, replete with hand-drawn rug, fireplace, sleeping pad, and magnetic flying saucer, all cut out of paper, with odds and ends and trinket-treasures placed here and there with the sort of attention to detail that comes from when a child's love and her creativity come together in a focused way.

There's just one problem: The flying saucer won't fit in Cuddle's house without obscuring the lovely rug. Nika wants to build Cuddles a garage for the flying saucer, which we do, using a mini milk carton, scissors, paper, a pen, and a pink crayon. Apparently Cuddles likes pink.

Then I tuck her in with kisses and pet her wonderful forehead. Her soft hazel eyes look up at me with the innocence of a baby. She tries to lick me like a puppy, as if sipping love droplets on my skin.

"Can we have a sleepover?" she inquires, expectantly. If she were an actual dog, she'd be letting her tongue hang out, while panting hopefully.

"I'll tell you what, I'll come in and join you for a sleepover after I do a few things and have a few minutes to chill out."

"Oh Mamasu. But I wish you could join me now!"

I got thinking how all creation is an act of separation, with the intent of connection. Out of oneness, the universe springs forth into a trillion unique expressions, all at the Word of God. Quantum physics lets us in on a secret: Each of us—every person, lake, and rock—is a unique composition of vibrations singing, consciously or not, a song to our Creator. It sounds so nice. The only problem with this situation is that we now have to deal with re-lationships, and even if that's the whole point, it isn't easy. I want something that conflicts with what you want. Someone wants you to do something and you would rather chew broken glass. Your kids want every ounce of lifeblood in you and they truly want it now. You would like to take your first shower in weeks, linger over a glass of wine on the deck, immerse yourself in a novel, or take a few hours to finish that work project that's important to you and if you have a boss, to her as well. We are all one, but we're not. Being unique expressions of God's creativity is cool, but what do you do when you feel the rub of it?

You become like your kidneys. Nobody talks much about the kidneys in public discourse. Metaphors of the heart and gut domi-nate conversation. "Follow your heart." "What's your gut feeling?" Whoever thinks to say "Manage your close relationships like your kidneys"? Your kidneys are brilliant at letting some elements in and keeping some out, depending on what's good for you. Levels of per-meability vary as well. The kidney knows that there is a time to let things flow in and a time to have clear boundaries.

I kiss Nika's head a bunch of times, wondering what my kidneys would do. Every survival instinct in me tells me to make a fast exit or my urgent desire for time to chill out won't happen. My kidneys tell me that there is a time to open up to the flow and a time to draw the line. I find a way that fits us in the moment.

"Nika, my sweet, beautiful girl, if you close your eyes and if you let yourself fall asleep right now, instead of chatting, I will stroke your hair and snuggle you as you drift off into dreamland. And then I'll go have a little time to myself and come back when it's my bedtime."

"Oh but Mamasu, I do so love to chat!"

"I know you do sweetheart. Nevertheless, if you want to fall asleep with me snuggling you, it will have to wait until tomorrow."

"Okay Mommy."

23

Sailing, Soccer, and Sex during Blue's Clues

October 14th, 2009

W *hoosh whoosh* is the sound outside my window as cars zip by on the wet roads. I find it soothing.

I've been feeling incredibly happy and overflowing with gratitude lately. Except for a few miserable days when I didn't feel like that at all. My father-in-law was in the hospital on his birthday for emergency cardiac surgery, my husband pissed me off so much I couldn't even fight with him until the next day, and I found myself reading doomsday theories about the year 2012. Everything seemed out of control. Even the weather pointed to the capricious side of life: little sprinkles of rain, then a downpour, then a sudden showing of blue sky, followed by gales of winds, and in turn, a peaceful, gentle moistness, like a calm blanket.

I like life when I cease controlling it. A sailor does not control the wind or the waves, but learns to artfully position his sails to influence the effect nature has on his course. A single soccer player cannot force everyone on the field to play out the ideal game she has in her head, but if she is agile, in the moment, and in tune with her teammates, she can influence the play—and the outcome. In our lives, there is fate and circumstance—the cards we are dealt, whether or not we chose them before birth. Once we are here, it's a wide-open playing field in which to engage, influence, and experience the fullness of life. Ultimately, you have to let go of control, or you miss out on the fun. Like with sex.

On the topic of sex, it's been a little challenging to find time to be alone. Often, when the kids are at school and my love is post-call, we've found our way into the lovely sheets, only to find a pair of yellow feline eyes staring curiously at us from under the bedspread. Privacy has become the ultimate intimate joke. The only thing to do is laugh and make love anyway. The other day, on a post-call weekend, my love and I put on a *Blues Clues* episode for the kids and snuck off into the other room. Unfortunately, the episode finished before we did. Our son busted through the lockless door and announced, "It's over!" Life cracks me up.

24

Emerging from Goo

October 15th, 2009

It's Tuesday and this evening my love and I have a little time to sneak out of the house like teenagers to enjoy hanging out with each other. Real teenagers sneak into the house, trying not to wake their parents. Grownup teenagers sneak out of the house, trying not to draw notice from their happily playing kids, who are sitting on the living-room floor playing Sorry! with the sitter.

My love and I find ourselves at Urban Grind, ordering a Local Pocket filled with something Indian, and a steamer. At the cash register, a picture of Princess Di stares cynically at the baked goods.

Local Pocket and steamer in hand, we head for our favorite black leather couch. Couches are perfect invitations for a high-PDA situation. The fact is, we've always been a high-PDA couple. Everyone has their own strengths. Ours has never been keeping our hands off each other, and not for lack of generic self-control. I was a virgin when I got married the first time. My love went from having partners in college to embarking on a seven-year period of intentional abstinence, starting the day he felt God's spirit warm his heart and ending the night he covered my bed in rose petals and promised to love me forever.

Our physical connection and spiritual connection have been effortless since the time my love and I first fell for each other. The friendship piece took longer to develop, in part because talking with caresses seemed so wordlessly perfect, like a language less cumbersome than English.

But as everyone who has ever fallen in love knows eventually you have to use your mouth for something other than kissing. You have to talk about whether to buy a house and what to buy for groceries and get honest about the things that have started to annoy you. Maybe the wet towels on the floor drive him a little batty because he hates mold. You may find it irritating that he buys whatever is on sale in bulk. If you don't talk about these things, they clog your romantic arteries; if you do, the spell is over and your lover is transformed from the image of beauty itself into a real-life person with a deep capacity to irritate you. And that's before you get to the crucible of your relationship. I suspect everyone has one: a particular issue or dynamic that won't go away if you ignore it, and seems impossible to solve using ordinary math. To get through the crucible, you have to use caterpillar math. Feed yourself with whatever nourishes you, then go into your chrysalis and become nothing. Sit with the gooey feeling of losing your entire identity. Let go of your old form. Let a force greater than your will re-create you into something that can fly. Something beautiful. You can't turn into a butterfly without first going through the goo stage.

For us, the med school years were the goo years.

I have no idea how, but with some help from somewhere, we emerged with wings. Wings that like to flutter and flirt. Wings that grow stronger with use. Occasionally we have to go through the goo phase from start to finish again, sort of like having the periodic cleansing diet that leaves your body in a new shape and healthier condition when you are finished. I once heard that the best marriages are remarriages to the same person. I totally agree. My love and I decide about every two to four years that the last time we said vows together we were pretty immature. So we write new vows and have a little wedding. First there was the wedding night we had when I was still legally married to someone else. We told our pastor ahead of time, along with a mentor and one or two friends. We made promises in the throes of consummating our love for the first time. A few years later, I wanted to see a doctor who was going to stop taking my insurance. We decided it was a good time to "tell the government that we are married," as we explained to our kids. It also felt like we had outgrown the first initiation into commitment and felt more ready to take our connection to a higher level.

I got a lovely dress with white and blue swirls off a sale rack, and we headed out to a special garden an hour away. Only a third of our immediate family was there, and my best friend from college got ordained online so she could officiate. Back at our condo, we danced with all our kids and with each other to a playlist off the computer. For food we had Mexican takeout on paper plates. I was nursing our youngest daughter at the time, so instead of wine, we had sparkling cranberry juice. I have a photograph of my love forming a dancing pyramid. I imagine we'll have another wedding in the future. It will probably be after the next goo phase leaves us feeling done with the old, on the cusp of lifting up on a fresh breeze with a spanking new set of wings. I hate to think of undergoing another goo phase, but it's inevitable.

The great thing is that through all the demons we have faced that we didn't want to at the time, my love and I have discovered the coolest thing: The more we let go of outdated versions of ourselves and submit to the goo phases that signify a season of transformation, the more confident we can be that out of the other side of the goo, we can be free to express who we really are on a new level, and it's totally worth it. The more freely we soar individually, the more irresistible we are to each other.

If we weren't meant for each other, it seems likely that growing would lead to growing apart. For us, the personal development we see in each other is extremely hot. The two of us are truly more in love with each other now than during the la-la phase of making goo goo eyes at each other. Nowadays when we look into each other's eyes, we aren't looking for someone to save us or shield us from insecurities. We are looking into the eyes of someone whose vulnerability we understand, whose flaws we know, whose strengths we admire, whose dreams we cherish, whose soul we recognize, and whose luscious physicality we love to touch, including on the couch at the coffee shop. Thankfully, these days we also have learned how to be friends, swapping stories, pondering insights together, playing Mad Libs, and tickling each other. I guess tickling is back to touching each other, but what I can say? I like my husband and he likes me. We have huge crushes on each other, and it's useless to hide it.

A young woman sitting across from us in a black leather chair looks up and smiles at us.

"You guys are cute."

"Would you be surprised to hear we have three kids at home?" I inquire.

"Yes I would. You certainly don't act like a couple that has three kids at home." I smile gleefully.

Everybody on earth has their own way of spreading light. One of the ways my love and I like to do it is by letting young people see us—happy and in love after plenty of challenges, including life with three young kids. So many young people are growing up inhaling the air of devastating splits and lukewarm marriages that keep going, but not like the energizer bunny at all. There are different forms of love, and I know of lovely individuals who have found true love with a dog or a grandchild, or as a volunteer for a worthy cause. I'm not deluded into thinking romantic love is the only important thing in life, or the only kind of fulfillment. But whatever the form, I think we all long for true love. The thing is, when we watch romantic comedies, or other non-tragic love stories on film, the credits predictably say when the two lovers overcome a few cheesy challenges they finally get together. Happily ever after, the end. You hardly ever see what happily ever after looks like. If I can reassure a few people that true love is possible, goo phases and all, it fills me with smiles on every inch of my insides.

My love and I chat with our new friend, Sarah. She's an art student at a nearby school, and she's dating a guy who is a massage therapist. My love mentions that he is an intern.

"That must be a lot of hours," observes Sarah.

"Yeah, but at least my program is pretty supportive. They don't try to abuse us on purpose, like I have heard they do in some residency programs."

When Sarah turns to me and asks what I do, I tell her about coaching.

"I've heard of life coaching," she says. "My boyfriend was telling me he met someone who he talked about doing a barter with for massage and life coaching."

"That's so funny. That was me!" I say.

It is such a very small world.

Sarah heaves her bag over one shoulder and heads off into the evening on her scooter. I love that she rides one. I think about how keeping a childlike whimsy, mixed with a little practicality, is so key to a life of celebration.

I hope Sarah and her massage therapist boyfriend are happy together. I can just picture them riding scooters into the sunset together.

25

Ice Skating

October 16th, 2009

I'm taking my oldest daughter ice skating today. Nika has the day off from school and she has been semi-begging to go with me for a while.

Normally I don't like malls. The florescent lights and the smell of too many scented candles and not enough fresh oxygen keep me shopping on Amazon every time. But the Lloyd Center, which is just a Max train ride away, has one cool feature: an ice skating rink in the center of the mall. Nika wants to ice skate with me because it is a point of connection. She knows that ice used to play a big part in my life. Nika knows I spent a great deal of my childhood gliding and spinning and leaping and landing on my butt in ice rinks. Which is why I didn't take my daughter ice skating until I knew she was too old to compete.

While I have some cool memories of my figure skating days, like when my Russian coach Galina would imitate my pour posture and say with her thick accent, "Alicia, Alicia, why look like bear?" and when I got to skate in a show with all the big stars, like Scott Hamilton, Ekaterina Gordeeva and Sergi Grinkov, and Oksana Baiul and Victor Petrenko, I saw enough anorexia to make me gag, and beyond that, I discovered that after spending a certain amount of time being "the girl with the amazing spiral," that even after I was ready to get on with getting a life, I was too afraid I couldn't do or be anything else that I clung to my skating world until I blew it enough times in competitions that my parents figured it was my unconscious way of saying "I don't want to do this anymore." How often do we cling to old roles and identities that no longer fit until some force outside ourselves gives us permission to quit by forcing us to let go?

I'm a huge fan of skating "just for fun." And tootling around the ice with my oldest daughter definitely qualifies as fun. I watch her go from clinging to the wall, to gripping my hand like a life preserver, to pushing off on her. Once she slips and falls and it looks like it may have been a bruiser.

"Are you okay?" I ask, offering a hand.

Nika looks me in the face and says, "I'm strong, I'm tough, and nothing can get to me."

After ice skating, Nika and I ride the escalator to the Food Court. We get a little order of cucumber sushi and a paper plate of super-greasy chicken teriyaki. On our way out, we split a strawberry smoothie, half of which we take on the road, in order to be on time to pick up Gabe and Avsi from preschool. In the car on the way over, I let Nika sit shotgun, in spite of the fact she is a little shy of the 60 pounds insisted on by Oregon's new car seat law.

Am I skating on thin ice?

26

48-Hour Getaway

October 16th, 2009

I'm curled in the crook of my husband's arm, nuzzling in and watching the downpour outside the window of the Cascades-Amtrak train we are taking, sans kids, to Vancouver, British Columbia. Thanks to my mom, along with one of my favorite neuroscientists/sitters, my love and I have 48 hours, including travel time, to sleep off our burnt-out stupor and live it up.

On the way to Canada, we sleep between train whistles for a while, and eventually we pull out our trusty Mad Libs, which we enjoy until the Seattle stop. We stretch our legs and look for some place to get coffee—after all, isn't that what you do in Seattle? It is a shocking disappointment to find that there isn't so much as a cappuccino dispenser, much less a world-class coffee shop, within walking distance from the train station. Oh well.

When the train gets going again, my love and I take out our own books and watch words pass by, along with the scenery out our rain-beaten windows. A little beach town called White Rock catches our attention. We file it away for future vacation reference.

Once we have de-trained, we chat with a nice naturopathic urologist who is in front of us on the way through customs. A nice

Canadian points us in the direction of the sky rail, which can take you just about anywhere, zooming about above the car traffic.

Once in the general vicinity of our accommodations, my love and I wander around downtown Vancouver until we find Hotel Mode, which is chic, interesting, and reasonably priced. In our room, a vase full of bright flowers has a note attached to it.

"I love you."

I pore over the note and welcome its contents, letting my love into the space of my heart.

In that shared space of deep, restful opening, my love and I enjoy the bed for sleep and other intimate purposes. By late morning, we find our way out into the fresh air of the new day in time to watch a rainbow birth itself through the cloud-heavy sky at Stanley Park.

On a whim, we walk into a salon and get Canadian haircuts. In the afternoon, we stroll around town and eat too much sushi and udon soup. It starts to rain again, and by the time we get back to our hotel, we are wet and my love is feeling a little ill to the stomach and I have a headache. He sleeps and I lay in bed watching the ceiling. For a little while, I slip into sleep too. At one or two in the morning, we wake up. My love is feeling a bit better, and after a little more fun without our clothes, it's time to go out. It doesn't matter that we still feel on the crappy side, physically. In a few hours, we'll have to leave the country. Why not *carpe diem*?

Even though the last thing our tired bodies need is a drink, my love and I step inside a little wine bar called Uva that is attached to our hotel. The two of us are curious about what a classy wine bar in British Columbia is like, our eyes and ears wide as we savor the ambience and watch the people. Instead of drinks, my love and I order tiny overpriced plates of fancy things.

As the time turns from late evening to the wee hours of morning, my love and I walk around the city, which is occupied by throngs of young people migrating in and out of clubs, almost like zombies responding to a homing device. It's fascinating to observe the nightlife from the safe and happy distance of a Blenz Coffee Shop, where we sip the most delectable dark hot chocolate imaginable.

At 4 a.m. we head back to our hotel to check out. Then we go back to Blenz to get another hot chocolate for the train ride home. At 5:30 a.m. we board our Cascades-Amtrak train and head home to Portland.

We find my mom, the babysitter, and our three kids at Tanner Springs. Avriana is pitching a loud fit. I hug the older two who want to be hugged, and watch Avriana from a safe distance. Twenty minutes later, her little arms stretch urgently upward toward me in the shape of an embrace. In a heartbeat, her whole self is wrapped around me like a koala.

27

Reentry

October 23rd, 2009

I'm lying on my pullout bed, listening to the sound of raindrops elucidating the quietness. The first quiet in a while. So many thoughts and feelings wash over me.

If the week following the weekend in BC were a film, the screen would be filled by open mouths screeching, fussing, relentlessly demanding more than I have in my inner bag of resources. My heart has been working to grow four sizes larger to include these sounds, this intensity in its beat of unconditional love. At the same time, my cortisol levels sit on my nerves like annoying relatives or low-level demons.

On Tuesday, I have my first coaching session with Cassi, my mentor. I want to focus on being more effective, with less effort. The single thread that emerges from our banter and reflection is "unconditional love." It's my highest calling, and I yearn to live it, show it, and impart it on an international scale. Doing that seems so far away when I'm being vetted by three little angelic beings who can get devilishly under my skin and inch me toward the cliff of insanity, where the choice between survival instinct and unconditional love so easily gets clouded by too much cortisol and the precipitous feeling that "you were on my last nerve 10 minutes ago."

When I get to that point, I go in the bathroom to cool off. It is the only room in our apartment with a lock. There is something about a mother who is crying or screaming in the bathroom that has a unifying effect on the kids. During the time leading up to a mommy-breakdown, no amount of strategic distractions, emotionally intelligent discussion of feelings and needs, or any rational attempt to find a mutually agreeable solution does an ounce of good. Even when I tell them it's in their best interest to let Mommy have a quiet minute or two in order to calm down, lest Mommy lose control and become a very wicked person, cooperation is not inspired. In fact, the expression of my own vulnerability typically inspires them to test to see if I'll really lose it. Even once I've locked myself up in the bathroom, they keep banging on the door, whining, fussing, copycatting, etcetera, until I scream. And then when their testing confirms that yes, push me hard enough and long enough and I will cry like a siren on a sinking ship, well then it finally clicks that I'm human. Only then does their compassion kick in. My oldest stops antagonizing her siblings and invites them into her room. The middle one stops whacking everyone and ruining their projects, and the little one stops dictating, on threat of tantrum, every little detail of what everyone else is supposed to do. Calm comes over the household. When I come out of the bathroom, catharses complete, I hear the sounds of three little people playing a peaceful game together in Nika's room. An angelic hand touches my face and asks me to read a story. A little body snuggles in. A sweet voice asks for an orange. A pair of hands rubs my shoulders. Empathic beings, all of them.

28

Presence

January 12th, 2010

I watched *Julie and Julia* last night with Ko. I had been told by at least four people that the way I'm writing myself through a year-long crisis reminds them in a heartwarming way of Julie. Julie is the character in the movie who blogs about cooking every recipe in Julia Child's *The Art of French Cooking* as a way to cope with, and possibly transcend, her life being not exactly as she imagined it would be at age 29 with 30 fast approaching. When my mother-in-law, who is also a writer, sent us the DVD after she watched it, leaving me happily without an excuse, I was thrilled.

The flick turned out to be inspiring and gritty, opening up the beauty, imperfection, and interconnectedness of individual lives, in the present and across time, as the imaginary presence of Julia leads Julie out of her own darkness, into her ratty little kitchen, and toward a life worth celebrating.

That said I have no more desire to bone a duck than I did 15 hours ago. On the other hand, I did choose to sit down and write today instead of a myriad of other things I could have spent time on during this opening of time. I'll admit a little influence there.

I'm at Lovejoy Bakers, looking out the glass walls at various passersby, when a pink blossom standing tall in its small, clear, square vase catches my attention. Its petals are thick, yet so alive you can almost see the atoms singing the flower into expression. I look long and hard at the pink blossom, oblivious to the hustle and bustle of customers buying bread and pastries and the chat of adults over the din of stroller occupants cooing and occasionally crying. Wordlessly, the thick pink petals outstretch themselves in an exclamatory "hello!" to whoever or whatever comes its way.

"Hi" I say back, under my breath. I have always had a thing for flowers. As a kid, when I learned that all flowers have to die, I cried for a long time. I like flowers even better than pets. I love the way flowers offer themselves up, like infinity opening itself before the eyes. Flowers also don't beg, sprinkle a trail of dirty litter across your bathroom floor, or sit on you at the most inconvenient times. Flowers simply exist as innocent expressions of life itself. They may not have the neurology of animals and people, yet they have presence. I cherish them for it.

Presence. Whoever was it that said of porn, "You know it when you see it"? You know "presence" when you feel it. You also know when you have shut it out, by its opposite, preoccupation. We can be preoccupied with an infinite variety of obsessions. For men, I think they start with insecurity and build everything else on that foundation. For women, we add worry and guilt into the mix, and then combine all three in every imaginable hybrid. For example, we make choices out of worry and insecurity, and then we guilt-trip ourselves for being so insecure and worried. Then we make new choices based on feeling guilty, and then we feel insecure. Then we worry. Often, we are so busy with worry and insecurity that we have no time to do anything other than juggle these three unwelcome relatives. Once in a while, we get enough of a helicopter view of our lives to see what a mess we have let these relatives make of them. This births a new preoccupation: regret.

There are countless things in our lives we wish we could undo. Where is the rewind button on our choices? The ones we really regret tend to fall into two categories of consequences: outcomes that happened or are happening now that could have been averted had we made wiser choices and outcomes that haven't happened or aren't happening now that we think could have if we had made wiser choices. It's easy to say "live and learn" when it seems like you and the people you care about are essentially no worse for the wear and you're happy with the overall outcome of things.

What do I regret? The thing I regret most is letting my youngest daughter scream and scream and scream until she had gnawed away the paint on her crib rail. At the time, things were not great with my love and I. At the time, I had two other intensely high maintenance children. At the time, I thought I was going to go insane, and that getting my daughter to sleep on her own at all costs would ultimately save us all.

Cry-it-out was hard on Nika, but by six months it was clear she wasn't going to fall sleep independently without a fight. At the time, I thought what I was fighting for was my first marriage. In any event, within a week, sleep training worked wonders on Nika's sleep habits. Once she got the hang of it, Nika slept a heavenly 12 hours. I had a freaking life, interrupted only by my own insomnia.

The same kind of sleep training worked less well with Gabe, but it worked to an extent. With my youngest, Avriana, cry-it-out was totally devastating, to us both. It didn't matter that I tried everything else imaginable, including climbing into the crib with her, practicing Martha Sears' secret "de-latch" technique after a nurse-to-sleep session (which never worked because Avriana always had her third eye open), and singing to her softly from across the room. My mother-in-law even got her a soft snuggly bear with a heartbeat recording in its tummy. It did nothing, though Gabe had fun opening the Velcro and removing the batteries. We created a predictable evening routine, including a soothing bath and a cuddly story time in a darkened room. Soft music, no music—it didn't matter. Every time I tried to leave, Avriana sensed it and woke up immediately.

The kid only wanted to sleep on my body, and I wanted my body back, for at least a few minutes at a time. I wanted a little time in the evening to myself, and I wanted to be able to sleep at night without being kicked, yanked, and grabbed every time rest seemed imminent. Time to at least minimally refuel my tank before another day of caring full-time for three high-intensity kids, each wanting every iota of my energy in totally different ways. I read that if you don't teach kids to sleep when they are little, they'll have sleep problems their entire lives. I figured I had to do something, for everyone's sake. My husband said that if I wanted his support in sleep training, I had to be committed. He was tired of my tireless ambivalence, trying this and that, hemming and hawing over parenting philosophies that come in neat little books that seem irrelevant to my situation, and wondering what to do and which priorities to prioritize. If I'm a shitty mother to all three of my kids because I'm totally burnt out is that better than if I inflict suffering on my child by making her cry-it-out? Or is it better to inflict suffering in the short term so that I can be a more present, loving mom in the long-term to each of my kids?

I was too stressed to listen to my intuition, and in a pinch, I made a call. I chose to inflict suffering, with the hopes that the end would justify the means. And I lost. More importantly, my little girl lost. Unlike my other two kids, who were more or less resilient and whose sleep did improve from the "training," Avriana screamed from the deepest part of her soul, the wounded cry of betrayal, which eventually turned to rage. I told myself I would not be weak like those moms who can't handle hearing the babies cry and cave in before sleep training has the chance to be effective. I cried. I left the house. I sung to her from the door. I watched for weeks as the sleep training failed, and in the morning, instead of a well-rested smiling baby, I saw a depleted face whose light had withdrawn. I had played the odds and lost. I tried to make it up to her by day, but anger had solidified in her, a rage that was not part of her original nature. I could not undo what I did. Insecurity over whether I did something wrong or passed on inferior genes to end up with kids who just can't seem to sleep turned to worry over what to do, and when all was said and done, then guilt took a seat front and center. With time, guilt mixed with sadness. Sadness mixed with regret. Regret mixed with longing to go back into the past and claim the daughter I felt I lost and do right by her, and that longing mixed with love for the little girl trying so hard to work through her anger. With love comes presence.

It's 2 a.m. and Avriana is awake and in a passionate funk. She is writhing on the floor, arching her back, and screaming if I get too close to her.

"Go away, Mom," she demands, throwing a vacuum cleaner attachment in my direction.

I give her space. I wait in the living room, letting my own tears fall. I watch her from a distance. Then I hear a snuffly little voice. "Mommy, can you come over here and dry my tears?"

I come over, sopping up her tears with my shirt, pressing firmly, yet lovingly, making sure to get the corners fully dry. I have learned from trial and error that how I dry her tears is as important as that I do it.

We sit quietly together in the hallway, a few inches outside the bathroom. Eventually we migrate to my bed, where we sit for a while, while I rock her. "Are you ready to lie down?" I ask.

"No. I want to sit in your lap!"

I reach for a glass of water. I sip it. I feel the sweetness of my little girl's trust occupying my lap.

"Can I have a sip of your water, Mom?"

"What's missing?" I say softly.

"Please," she whispers.

"Of course. Here you go."

"After you have a sip of water, can we lie down? Mama is very sleepy." I can hardly keep my head from flopping forward, my droopy eyes open, but I know this is important. If I force her too fast, we'll be back where we started.

Avriana looks at me with her wide wise eyes, an old soul from the beginning.

"Yeah. First I'll have a sip of water. Then lie down and snuggle me."

In the morning, inside my ear, I hear a little voice whisper, "I love you Mama." On her own internal cue, Avriana hops happily off the bed.

Presence cannot fix a thing for another person, but it has a way of fostering the unconditional conditions in which a person is freed up to fix it themselves.

29

A Circle with Legs

January 14th, 2010

Here is the history of tables I have owned up until today. First, there was my ex's bachelor table for two, which was made out of ugly, cream-colored plastic, with metal legs. When I moved into my own apartment with little Nika, my mom gave us a lovely, round, wooden children's table that had been used in the nursery school she ran from her house for a few years. Nika and I are little people, and when my love started sharing meals with us, he squeezed in too, without complaint.

When the three of us moved to Jersey for the kickoff of med school, my mother-in-law graciously gave us her old kitchen table, which we hoisted onto the U-haul truck we used to get our things from Massachusetts to Jersey. That little old table did well by us considering the circumstances. However, after enduring the sticky hands of three toddlers, for Nika was just under two when we bought our condo just outside of Cherry Hill, the chipping paint was embedded with unrecognizable dried goo. The goo was no match for a scraping knife. It was time to lay the gooey table in a dumpster side burial.

When we first moved to Oregon, the economy was still tight, and we were carrying our Jersey-bound mortgage, along with our monthly rent in Portland. It wasn't exactly the time to go out and buy a table. So we went back to using the circular, wooden kids table that Nika first colored on back in Acton, Massachusetts. After my love and I sold our condo in Jersey, we kept using the kids table. Because whatever disposable income we had quickly got gobbled up by preschool tuition, family frozen yogurt outings, happy-hour nibbles on evenings out for just the two of us, and of course on my two fundamental financial weaknesses: fresh supplies of books and fair trade chocolate. I figured why buy an El-cheapo table to replace an El-children's table when you know someday you'll probably be able to get a table you actually like, or possibly adore. My love thought that way of looking at the table situation made sense.

But options and opinions sometimes change quickly when new information comes in. My love and I heard that Portland is home to a ginormous IKEA. Not only that, we heard that IKEA has lovely, yet inexpensive tables. So we went to have a look, and lo and behold, on the top floor of IKEA, our entire family met its first honest-to-goodness table. Inspecting the light-colored, round pine table with a built-in leaf, it was love at first sight for four out of the five of us.

Initially Avsi said, "I don't like that one." A moment later, her facial expression adjusted itself and she said, "I do like that one." Avsi's friend Finnigan at school commented the other day, "Avsi says no, then she says yes." Avriana must have internalized that observation, because looking at the IKEA table in front of us, she noted her own reaction: "I said no; then I said yes."

The table didn't fit in our Prius, so we had to drive off with only the chairs. Thankfully, the world's cutest couple, Erin and Darin, offered to pick up the table for us and bring it over in their Subaru SUV.

When they first dropped the table on the living-room floor, I thought that was it. Then Erin and Darin saw the glazed look fall across my face as they described in chipper tones the "simple" steps involved in putting it together. "Do you want us to set it up for you?" Erin finally asked. "Cause we can totally bang this out in 10 minutes. We just didn't want to deprive you of the fun of it." I gratefully accepted the offer, reassuring them that I will have more fun witnessing the miracle of our table taking shape than by participating in that miracle directly.

The last screw has just gone in, and Erin and Darin have brought a circle with legs to life.

At last, a table of our own.

30

The Line

January 16th, 2010

The line between happiness and its opposite is like a tightrope—flexible, wobbly, and thin as air. It's the invisible space between thoughts before action. It's the interpretation of our lives in the shadowy zone where past experience swirls with sensory input, personal values, free will, and the hormones of the day, to weave the story we tell ourselves and what it means. It's the ultimate intersection of fate and choice.

I'm teetering back and forth on that line, and I feel like I'm going to take a fall. My love has just inquired about what kind of childcare I want for this weekend when he's on-call, again. It's nice of him to want to help secure the childcare so I can have a break for an hour or two while he is at the hospital.

Intellectually, I know he's trying to do a good thing for me, trying to be the good guy, the good partner, but you know, I don't fucking care.

I care, but what I mean is I'm trying to do these little things to try to mitigate how unfair this whole thing is, but it's making me angry right now, like he is trying to put a band-aid on an internal bleed and tell me everything is fine.

My husband arrived home in time for lunch today, after being away all day and all night. He considers getting home in time for lunch getting home in the morning if lunch occurs at or before noon. I hate when my husband slants his interpretation of his schedule to make it seem less infuriating. I'm all for optimism, but this brand of it feels a whole lot more like a slap in the face, like when my love and I were first getting serious and he informed me residency would be a lot easier on us than in the past since he'd only have to work 80 hours a week instead of the old traditional workload of 120 or more hours.

Of course, I know my love feels helpless too. I know he loves me and would do anything in his power to make me happy, and it simply isn't in his power to erase his own calling or to alter the shape of hoops one has to go through to get qualified for a calling like medicine. So he does what he feels is in his power, and he hopes, against all odds, that it will ease my upset. The only person who can truly make me happy, though, is me. I know it. I see the line.

I see the line wobbling too, as I ruminate on how I don't really feel like thinking about the next damned time my love will be missing out on family time, or his well-intentioned efforts at making things better by contracting his job of being there to a babysitter. It's especially hard being married to someone who is only occasionally and sporadically around to hang out or share the work of parenthood when tons of neighborhood dads come out of the woodwork wearing baby slings and squatting next to their wide-eyed young children staring at the orange and silver fish in the water at Tanner Springs. I knew my love feels more that he was chosen for the work of medicine than that he chose it, yet it is achingly tempting to wish he could be one of those dads. Of course, that's impossible, because to erase my love's calling to medicine would be to fundamentally change who he is. And I love him more than I lust the idea of my ideal life and parenting partner. Maybe I should create one of those boyfriends-in-a-box, pin my love's face on it, and imagine that I can bridge that chasm between the one I love and the way of life I long for with that one.

I try to keep an even tone that sounds professional enough to hide the tears that are lurking under my lids, as I inquire, "Are you on-call Saturday or Sunday?"

"Saturday."

Saturday call totally screws the weekend. He leaves fairly early in the morning, works all day, works most of the night, and comes home on Sunday just before lunchtime, with 1 or 2 hours of sleep behind him.

I cringe and feel myself losing balance.

The tightrope is swinging beneath me as I indulge in the female tendency to see the big picture. I'm thinking not only of this coming Saturday, but of all the weekends, past, present, and future, that get eaten into, without my consent. I stomp my foot, knowing my husband can't see it from the other side of the table. The burn of tears is looming, accompanied by the temptation to walk up to my love and say, "Just so you know, I'M UPSET!"

In the same nanosecond of temptation, in that itsy-bitsy invisible space between my neurons, I sense that arguing with the unchangeable aspects of life is a no-win proposition. The facts of internship are the facts, unfortunately. As much as every iota of my being wants to tear down the institution of medical education and work with other outside-the-box innovative thinkers to create a saner and more flexible and effective way of training doctors, no one has asked for my opinion or my coaching services. And with my husband being on the bottom of the totem pole as an intern, he doesn't get much more say than I do. It is hard to surrender a battle, even if you know it is a losing one.

In this case, I lose bigger if I fight, which is contrary to my nature. Surrender is so hard. Our weekends oscillate in form, length, and structure, and in that, if I can let go, is a freedom to improv with life. I can love it or fight it, celebrate it or hate it.

I walk out the door into a crisp, lightly raining day, each inhale and exhale quivering through me as I walk the line between tears and freedom, misery, and opportunity.

A guy who lives in our building is smoking a cigarette and sipping coffee under the overhang of our building's entrance. I know him by face, but not by name.

"I gotta hand it to you ... running a household, husband's an intern ... you're one in a million. Your kids are great. Your husband's doing well, isn't he? Really, I gotta hand it to you, balancing life like you do ..."

I comment about the ongoing dance of finding that balance, the dynamic equilibrium. I wonder at the fresh air and the fresh tears I could easily manufacture and the encouragement in the face of this guy.

"The whole of life is a dance, isn't it?" he says.

"Yes it is," I say, feeling my footing become more assured underneath me, for the moment, at least.

As I wait for the orange hand on the signal light to turn white, so I can walk across the street to Lovejoy Bakers, I look up at our apartment window and the most joyful thing happens: Faces and smiles and little outstretched fingers and voices calling out "I love you Mommy!" "Have a wonderful day Mom!" "I love you. Bye Mommy."

My heart swells with joy as I wave wildly and call to them and jump up and down on the sidewalk without a care as to what passersby may think. Even though I'm walking away, inwardly I feel intimately in synch with the little people I love. When you are a parent, one of the sweetest things is a happy farewell, knowing that your connection is thriving, your kids are happy, and you can enjoy the time apart as an opportunity to collect stories to tell in the car at pickup, or at the table of togetherness, whenever two or more are gathered.

Like fog lifting, life is clearing up today, and it sure is easier to walk the line in front of you when you can see the way ahead.

The fog will surely come back, but it will clear again too, like a day in San Francisco.

31

The Power of a Shower

January 18th, 2010

U pon waking, I hear the shower going. A small exception is
made to the universal laws that govern waking up in the Kwon
family, which normally prohibit me from sneaking out of bed without either Gabe or Avriana rising to follow me wherever I may go.
On tiptoe, I make my way toward the bathroom, open the shower
curtain to find a naked man, and more importantly, the naked man
who is the love of my life, dripping wet in front me. I hop in with
him and let the shower pour its strands of water over my body like
water spaghetti. My love lathers me up with soap and rinses me and
wraps me in a towel.

It's Monday. It is a holiday, I think. No school for the kids. My
love still has to work. No big surprise, but still a bummer.

I stand there in a daze for a minute, my brain still fuzzy, trying to
orient myself, and in that 60 seconds, my love slips into scrubs and
is off to work. If I weren't still draped in the towel, his own hands
placed on me, it would be easy to have dismissed the few precious
moments of lathered togetherness as a figment of my imagination.
I smell the remnants of lavender soap bubbles on my skin, a little
fragrant connection to linger on with me as I start the day, which
I'm not ready to start. Since the miracle of sleeping kiddoes is still

in progress, I mosey back into bed. It's only 6:05. In a few minutes, the kids start rubbing their eyes and elongating their little bodies into shapes resembling starfish. Yet the bending of cosmic law continues in a way.

Usually the first thing that happens when the kids wake up is that they are hungry and they don't want anything that they could get themselves, or any of the first five things I offer. Often Gabe is nonstop fussy for no apparent reason, like someone forgot to replace his batteries and he just can't turn off the annoying sounds. Trust me, if I knew what batteries would lend peace to that boy and to our house, I would stock up for a lifetime. As it is, I try to sneak extra amino acids, like tryptophan, into his food, load him up with omega fatty acids that come in a yummy syrup, and hope for the best.

If Gabe's problem is that he is fussy for no particular reason and doesn't know what will help him feel better, Avsi has the opposite issue. Often she wakes up annoyed for a specific reason and knows with the precision of an engineer exactly what she wants and has little tolerance when the people who love her don't quite get it right. If Nika is up, it's only due to the noise, which means she is liable to be grumpy because the last thing she wants is to be awake.

Yet today, the kids loll about on top of me like happy cubs. I think they are imagining I am an island and there is an ocean all around. I let them play, interfering only to cuddle, kiss, and blow occasional raspberries on them periodically.

They wait for at least 20 minutes before asking me for a thing. Oh happy day, when I get to stretch into a starfish, happily and peacefully cuddle my cuties, and enjoy the innocent wonder of a fresh morning before the cute offspring unconsciously flick the switch into on-demand mode.

I finally get up and fetch wanted things for various people: vitamins, undies, waffles.

After breakfast, while I check email and catch up on work and check email again, Gabe climbs on my back, dives over my shoulder, into my lap, and coos, "You're such a cute, amazing mom!" I love you!"

I close up my computer and snuggle that little boy. "'Cause you can do that later," Gabe says, explaining the rationale of my choice out loud.

Following weeks of constant clouds, a festival of blue sunny skies stretches out overhead as our day unfolds, a blank slate to live on.

The clear aqua heavens streaked with white and gray mist comes with a clear message, which is not hard to decipher: Go outside immediately before the sun is obscured!

It's easier to coordinate an entire party for adults than to facilitate getting this group of little people out the door, prioritizing which whims to honor and when to risk a tantrum, finding shoes that like to go missing, helping out with last-minute potty needs, and outfitting everyone for the ever-changing weather. Finally, we make it out and the sun smiles at us with a wink of pleasure.

Nika brings a big pink, white, and black basketball given to her by an old sitter. Avsi carries her very own pink and purple soccer ball, along with a nativity statue of Mary and the Baby Jesus, which she discovered in the shoe bin. Gabe brings one of his many sets of keys.

Our foursome walks over to the dog park, just past Tanner Springs, where there is a wide-open field and a yellow statue that looks like a piece of abstract art that someone created on the computer and then turned into a three-dimensional cutout.

Nika, Gabe, Avriana, and I kick the two balls around for a while. Kick, chase. Kick, pass. Kick, pick it up with your hands. It's fun to frolic. Fun to kick. Fun to watch the enthusiasm of a child's foot finding the ball and sending it on a journey of cause-and-effect. We breathe in the loveliness of fresh light-filled air, and when we have had enough kicking of balls in the park, we collectively trot over to Lil' Green Grocer, where we pick out some apples and raisins and our favorite rainbow rice noodles: the colorful, thin, curly ones.

I chat with the owner, who is a great guy, whose wife travels frequently for work.

"How was your weekend?" I inquire.

"It was great. Susie had to work, so I got to spend some time with the girls. We had a lot of fun."

The guy's face twinkles. Clearly this father isn't faking it. He isn't trying to convince himself that, in spite of his wife being away, he's had a great time with his kids. He's convinced. He doesn't need to sell himself a comforting version of his reality, because he has already chosen a way of interacting with the facts of his situation that makes his face twinkle.

As we wind our way circuitously through Tanner Springs on our way home, I'm introspective. I think about the Lil' Green Grocer guy. He had two options on the table. That guy could have said, "Oh the weekend was a little long. Nancy was away, so I was on my own with the kids, but ya know, we hung in there and made the best of it," which is the polite way of saying it actually sort of sucked a little, or maybe a lot. But that's not what the Lil' Green Grocer guy did. He picked a different story line to shape his weekend: "It was great. Susie had to work, so I got to spend some time with the girls. We had a lot of fun."

I make it back to our place in time for a coaching teleclass. The kids, against all odds, are unheard and unseen for a full hour! When I hang up the phone, we put on *Miracles Happen* and prance around the living room.

Having worked up an appetite, Avsi, Gabe, Nika, and I snack on turkey, kiwi, and other nibbles before heading out on our one planned expedition for the day: a trip in search of New Cascadia Traditional (Gluten Free) Bakery. Ever since we found out that all four of us are allergic to gluten, we have been a little bummed, Nika and I in particular. We love our starch and our sugar. Oh, the chewy part of bread! Finding out about New Cascadia is like seeing a ray of hope within reach of our salivating tongues.

My love has left directions to the gluten-free bakery in the front seat of the Prius. I pick them up, trying to decipher the words through the sunlit page. Even for a doctor, my love's handwriting is bad. Nika is giving him lessons in penmanship. At age seven and a half, she has the prettiest writing in the family at this stage of the game.

I find my way surprisingly easily up and down several ramps and roads, and in fewer than 10 minutes the four of us pull up across from New Cascadia Traditional (Gluten Free) Bakery.

Everyone is thrilled, except for Gabe, who is in one of those moods where he doesn't want anything. Nika and I exchange a few looks. We have learned to take the waves less seriously and it's easier that way. I click a picture of the New Cascadia sign, and the kids in front of it, to show my love later. We have been looking for a gluten-free bakery for so long it feels like finding a long-lost relative. We cross the street, open the doors, and stare, with our mouths dropping off of our chins, at the loveliest gluten-free confections imaginable: impeccably frosted, ever-so-moist cupcakes; four kinds of cookies; essence of lemon scones; fresh-basil-garnished pizza; even gluten-free hamburger buns.

We settle on a pizza, a scone, a pumpkin-quinoa muffin, and a triple chocolate brownie. Everyone shares everything joyfully. Even Gabe cheers up and relaxes when the food comes. From the first lip-smacking bite to the last, each treat melts in our mouths. It is so good, we eat mostly in silence. Nika's face shines like a million suns with the thrill of being in a place where the phrase "You can't have that, it has wheat in it" doesn't exist. Her whole being emanates with the jubilant satisfaction of YES, even while Gabe oscillates between peace and fussiness like a radio oscillating between song and static.

Then we play a game of Mad Libs and discuss forming a new tradition of New Cascadia on days when Daddy's on-call and I get to spend some time with the kids. Avriana uses the potty on her own terms and stays 100 percent dry the entire outing.

The kids and I enjoy passing the afternoon watching *Charlotte's Web*. It was the first film I took Nika to see in the theater when she was five. As Charlotte weaves her magic words, it strikes me that Wilbur's fate rests on a matter of perception. Is he a runt? Or is he "Some Pig"? I love Charlotte's observation to Wilbur that the title "Some Pig" isn't about something you *do*, it's something you *are*.

Once the kids are in bed, I open up my laptop—the one I closed when Gabe sought my undivided lap earlier—and when I open up my yahoo account, an email is waiting for me:

"Sweet love, I was just thinking of you and actually I was thinking about you most of the day ... I was so happy when you joined me in the shower this A.M. I knew I would be late for sign-out and I chose to wash your lovely hair and beautiful body anyway, and I am so glad I did!"

If someone asked me how my Monday was, I'd say, "My husband was out working, so I got to spend some wonderful time with the kids. It was lovely."

And I wouldn't have to sell myself the story, because I already lived its truth, and now that truth lives inside me.

32

Oh Shit

January 22nd, 2010

Everyone has "Oh shit" moments. Admit it. Even you. Or perhaps, especially you. The last 48 hours have offered up a lifetime record of "Oh shit" moments in a two-day period.

OH SHIT MOMENT #1

It's 8:09 and I'm walking back from the coffee shop to meet up with our great sitter, who in theory, has already taken my oldest and her carpool buddy to school. I'm ready for the handoff of the little ones so we can get on the road to preschool.

Sitter: "I don't know where Nika is. She and Lilly said something about not wanting to go to school, and I spent the last 15 minutes looking for them and calling their names in stairwells and I can't find them."

Me: *"Oh shit."*

Sitter: "I looked all over the apartment, then I locked up and went up to Cami's place, and her mom said the girls were there but they left."

Me: *"Oh shit."*

I run like I haven't run since I was 10 up five flights of stairs and knock three times, LOUDLY on Cami's door, thinking *oh shit, oh shit, oh shit,* until finally Jimmy, the live-in middle-age boyfriend of Cami's mother, answers the door in a towel.

Me: "Are the girls here?"

Jimmy: "I took them. They're at school. I dunno ... I guess I got confused because of Late Opening yesterday. They came up, so I just took them. I can take them again tomorrow."

Me inside my head: Really? I went through all that because you got confused about Late Opening? *Oh shit.* Seriously?

Me, out loud: "All right, thanks a lot Jimmy. Have a good one."

I find my way downstairs and out to the garage, where the sitter had very nicely gotten the little ones strapped in, and I hug her with relief and make comments like, "Whew, enough drama for today," and off she goes to work.

OH SHIT MOMENT #2

I get in the car and in one second I realized the sitter still has my keys. *Oh shit.*

I leap up, lock the car so no one can take the tots strapped inside, and dash off after the sitter, thinking I can easily catch up with her—it's only been one second or two or three and she works a few blocks down the street. The sitter is not in sight. I dash around the immediate neighborhood like a woman on crack, peering in all the coffee shops, in case she decided to grab a latte before work. No sign of the sitter, or my keys, and my car is locked, with two out of my three kids in it.

Oh shit.

After racing back to the side of my children, I find my presence of mind enough to remember that Gabe is in fact not a baby anymore, and that we recently switched to the seatbelt-only booster.

I belt out as loud as I can through the window: "Sweetie, can you unlock the door for me?"

YES! He can reach the lock! Phew! Wow. Thank God. What a day. Phew. Wow.

OH SHIT MOMENT #3

It's early evening and the babysitter is due to come within 5 minutes to relieve me for an hour. All of a sudden, I hear a small, plaintive, semi-whining, somewhat demanding voice implore, "Mom, clean me up." I follow the voice's trail until I reach Avsi, whose foot is literally dripping with liquid poop.

Oh shit.

I grab a paper towel and evacuate her immediately into the bathroom for emergency cleanup and an impromptu bath. The mission is messy, smelly, and challenging, but at least she's standing there compliantly while I wipe and wet and wipe some more until her bum no longer looks like a dripping mud castle or a leaky mustard bottle. I plop her in the now perfectly temperate bath and return to the site of the incident for further investigation and action-planning.

Ugh. I heave and come within an inch of vomiting. This is the worst, most fowl, vile poop of all my kids, ever. It has a solid center, surrounded by a lake of brown, noxious goo, like a lava cake gone to crap.

Oh shit.

Sure I used to puke changing diapers when I was pregnant, but I am totally not preggo, unless one of the country's top urologists somehow butchered a standard vasectomy and lied about the six-week follow-up sample coming back clean. Not that you needed to know that, like at all.

I run from the room, gulp down a huge quantity of air, grab my camera, and take a picture of the specimen, in order to show, or at least threaten to show, my daughter's future boyfriends. Next, I hold my breath, and pinch my nose with one hand, while frantically stripping the sheets and pillowcases off the incident site. Nika is looking on, with one eyebrow raised, with combined empathy, concern, and subtle amusement.

"I hope you're going to be okay," she says.

"Oh I will be," I reply, continuing the strip-fest at least as fast as the speed of sound, until everything horrifying is at last tied up in a black trash bag. I let my breath out.

I look for quarters to get a wash started. None in sight.

Oh shit.

This *Oh shit* moment is less inflammatory, less potent, more like an afterthought or an "It figures."

The crap is sealed off the black trash bag, the crapper is happily playing in the water-filled tub with little flakes of feces floating around, and the sitter should be here any minute.

When she arrives, *Oh shit* turns into *Oh well,* as I kiss each kid and walk out the door, into the evening air, cooled by the rain.

33

Love Lessons from IKEA

January 23rd, 2010

This evening, all five of us Kwons are going to spend Friday night like a good American family: shopping. Ordinarily, we shun a lot of things that typical American families do: We don't get TV reception or cable, only one of us has a cell phone, and instead of purchasing a spacious home in the suburbs, we have elected to pack our family like sardines into a little two-bedroom rental downtown, just for starters. We make a concerted effort to avoid Wal-mart, we never shop the day after Thanksgiving, and the only time we eat fast food is on vacation in California, when we load up on In & Out's protein-style veggie burgers, which doesn't include a burger of any kind—it's just lettuce, ranch dressing, and little bits of greasy onion. We don't own a Wii or any other video game system, we don't spend our weekends on home-improvement projects (because neither of us knows how to fix stuff), and we don't get our kids a new wardrobe in preparation for the first day of school. We don't watch football either, and although we used to go to church, we don't anymore ... because we are unrepentant sinners.

Tonight we are living the American Dream. After an enjoyable, yet long day spent mostly with the kids, and partly on part-time work, the wife embraces her husband who has just come home after spending 12 or more underpaid hours doing a job that involves both menial and meaningful aspects. The children attach themselves to their daddy's legs and arms, and everyone is quite visibly together. This peaceful reunion lasts approximately 30 seconds, whereupon the unified entity disentangles itself and various little and big people start moving in different directions, with divergent intentions.

The parents' intention is obvious: to have everyone immediately and peacefully put on their shoes and sweatshirts for a quick exit out the door, so we can get to IKEA before it closes, and leave in time to get the kids back in their beds before the clock strikes the witching hour, at which point tomorrow would be destroyed before it even arrives.

Nika's intention is to continue reading her book, plain and simple. Avsi wants everyone to attend an imaginary wedding, and she intends to wear mismatching shoes. And Gabe is driving a lone train in circles around a small area of the living room, completely immersed. He is living intention with irritating abandon.

"Are you ready, Gabe?" I ask, trying to sound patient.

"Not yet," Gabe responds resolutely.

It's after his *bedtime,* for goodness sake.

My love and I smile as we watch the old-man expression form on Gabe's little angelic yet curmudgeonly face.

At long last, we are out the door, Avsi still in her mismatched sandals. Fifteen minutes later, we enter IKEA-land: bedroom walls with secret tunnels that give way to other perfectly coordinated rooms for every sensibility, from ultramodern to psychedelic. The kids plop themselves on various beds, half tired, half hyper. It seems like we have only just begun explorations when, without a single item on our shopping list checked off, the loudspeaker crackles on and a voice announces, "IKEA will be closing at 9 o' clock, which is in 15 minutes. Please make your final selections and proceed to the checkout line. IKEA will reopen tomorrow at 10 a.m."

By half a miracle, my love and I find the most important items we came for: a comforter and duvet spread to replace the improperly fitting futon cover that is a royal hassle to put on every single day when we rise and take off every night when it's time to fall asleep.

I ordered the improperly fitting cover on impulse when our old futon cover started looking so bad I was embarrassed to have people over, and I couldn't find any replacement covers designed for our futon. I was tired and annoyed and had PMS, so I just closed my eyes, hoped all futon covers might be created equal, and purchased it. It was more a leap of denial than a leap of faith, and I've regretted it ever since.

I'm feeling like I can finally put that whole thing behind me now that I have in hand a lovely and inexpensive alternative that will add both ease and beauty to my life, for only $14.99.

Also on the IKEA list: a nice plant. Increasingly, I've felt a longing to green the apartment, literally. There is something about having lush plant life growing inside that makes a place feel soothing and uplifting. Just as the final warning is issued from the IKEA loudspeaker, I find the ideal green friend: a tall, slender plant comprised of several roots entwining upward together and bright leaves shaped like flower petals. I'm sold, literally. On the way to checkout, I grab a breakfast-in-bed tray and a side-sleeper pillow.

When I planned this evening sojourn to IKEA and back, I figured everyone would sleep in the car on the ride home. How untrue that fantasy is turning out to be. Everyone is wide awake and in finicky moods. While my love un-straps Gabe and Avsi, I load all of our loots into my arms and head for the door, planning to hold it open for my love, while he helps get the kids inside. Avriana specifically asked for Daddy to help her out of the car, so I'm thinking, Good, I'll help with the parts of this picture that don't fuss or demand unreasonable things at unreasonable hours. Of course, once I'm two-thirds of the way to the door, I hear what sounds like a cross between an angelic little girl and a screeching police siren: "Mommmmmmy."

At this point, I know that parental pleading is completely pointless.

Usually it's easier to go with the flow, which is the last thing I want to do, since I have the same fiery spirit as my daughter.

I do what I don't want to do, and carefully hand off my armload of stuff to my partner in IKEA-shopping and extract our alert daughter from her seat. Avsi unfolds herself and snuggles warmly into my torso as we traverse the garage, swipe our FOB, and open the door that leads to the lobby. I hold the door open.

I start to wonder, did my husband manage to lock himself in the car, what with the childproof locks? Things invariably take longer when my love is involved. I tend to operate on hyper-drive and he tends to take a slower pace. When I'm feeling in a happy mood, I say he is easier going. When I'm annoyed, I say he putters around. But how much putter can one man do in a vehicle with two children and some stuff from IKEA? I mean I know it takes a long time to put IKEA items together, but usually one waits until inside the home to do that, and besides, we haven't purchased anything that requires assembly.

An unheard of amount of time with no sign of Gabe, Nika, or my love ... I'm trying to be patient.

"Are you coming, sweetie?" I ask in as nice a voice as I can muster, considering my bewilderment at the holdup.

"Yes, we are coming." A strain is in my love's voice. I can feel my own tension rise. What right does he have to be grumpy and snappy when I'm waiting here, holding the door open with a heavy toddler in my arms, with no update on why it's taking a ridiculous amount of time.

Nika appears with an "uh-oh" look on her face.

"Um, there was a lit-tle accident with the plant," she explains.

I feel a sinking feeling. Why do things seem to go wrong when I let other people handle important things for me? Why, *in particular*, do things seem to go awry when I let *my love* handle important things for me?

I know it's not *about* the plant. Of course it's about layers of a lifetime of disappointment, of feeling like I can't count on others, that I have to do everything myself or else it gets screwed up, of feeling like I can't entrust something vulnerable, whether my actual soul, or an IKEA plant, into the hands of another person. It's about unfulfilled expectations and incalculable letdowns. It's about being tired of internship and being tired of feeling letdown and just plain tired. In spite of such awareness, I'm really upset about the plant, specifically.

I love that plant. I bonded with it in the store. Why did it have to be the newly beloved plant that had a little accident? Why not his stack of papers on obscure childhood diseases and their treatment protocols that sits precariously on top of our bookcase, untouched, and not nearly as lovely as a lush green plant with intertwining roots?

Disappointment is a tricky emotional experience to navigate because it cannot be denied without being plunged underground to fester. Once it festers, disappointment turns into more toxic compounds, made from molecules of self-pity, blame, rage, resentment, and learned helplessness. You don't want to be around, the pressure builds, and the volcano of such compounds explodes. You also don't want to *be* that exploding volcano. Trust me, I know. I once shattered a mug my love made for me during such an eruption. What was even more surprising is that he in turn broke the one I had made for him. As he is the more "even" member of our team, his lava must have been percolating for a long time. Even if you are a nice person, *especially* if you are a nice person, you cannot keep a lid on it forever.

The key, I'm learning, is to let emotions pass through without fueling them. If I'm disappointed, better to feel the rain than to add lightning and strike down a living tree. If I'm feeling anger, better to experience the thunder than to add hate and evoke a tornado that destroys everything in its path. If I'm feeling letdown, better to sit with it in a wet puddle than to drown the person I love in one inch of muddy water.

I see the damage to my precious plant is bad. The bulb and roots are completely out of the soil, most of which is on the cement floor of the garage. I cringe and feel the quivery sensation of tears.

Inside, once our IKEA stuff has been set down and the little ones are settled and tucked in for the night, I take a closer look at the plant to see how much earth it has lost, how mortal or superficial its wounds might be, to get a sense of whether it is a total loss, or something salvageable with a little TLC. At the moment, the wish to heal the plant is stronger than my irritation and disappointment in my partner.

Nika, my oldest, is full of inquiry and concern. I can feel her absorbing my emotions, identifying with me, watching how I handle myself, how I interpreted the situation. I hear in my head, and in the whirl of my feelings, the story I could tell, and it's not a pretty one. I can't think of a better story to tell, so I do something unlikely: I listen.

My love admits he had a feeling that it was too much to carry everything all at once. He explained how he tried to grab the breakfast-in-bed tray from the trunk to add it to the things I had handed off to him when I needed my arms to get Avsi. I can tell he sees in my face how sad and upset I am. He is sorry about what happened, sorry he didn't listen to his intuition, sorry that I am so sad. My love offers to scour the garage for additional dirt that might help save the plant, along with promises of a foot rub. The poor guy, he is an amazing guy, and he is trying so hard.

So I say to Nika, "Everyone sometimes doesn't listen to their intuition. We all do things that aren't the wisest. Like remember when I bought that futon cover that didn't fit properly? I had a feeling it wouldn't work. I just *wanted* it to fit, so I wouldn't have to deal with it anymore, so I went ahead and got it. We all make mistakes, honey."

Come to think of it, what I did with the futon is probably a bigger leap of stupidity and lack of wisdom than trying to carry an entire IKEA load in one trip. Humility is a helpful revelation.

When my love comes back with a handful of dirt from the garage, I transfer the unearthed plant into a new pot and lovingly pat the dirt surrounding it until the earth and roots seem solidly connected enough to have the opportunity to merge. As I press the earth gently, one last time, I ask You-Know-Who to fill me with unconditional love, which I send to the plant and to my love.

When I'm finished patting and praying, I look up. My love and I are alone in the kitchen.

My love opens up his shirt and extends his arms in an invitation to come inside and get wrapped up in the soft snuggle of a hug.

I choose love. I choose *him*, the one I love. I let love be more important than holding onto the disappointment, which I let go. Letting go feels ... well, like love. Happy, freeing, powerful in its powerlessness, like dissolving into something much more wonderful than your old idea of you.

Smiles have a way of taking over entire bodies, and so it is as my smile spreads from head to toe as I kiss my husband, confident in the knowledge of the things I can do. I can repot plants and pat love into them. I can choose to love, rather than to fight. And sometimes I can avert the fight by simply feeling what's there, looking at it, letting it pass on through, and opting for love in the present tense.

So far, the repotted plant is thriving. I'll keep an eye on it.

34

The Upside of Getting Stuck in the Mud

January 25th, 2010

I'm looking for a spot to park at New Seasons, which is a go-local, funky version of Whole Foods. I spy a spot close to the entrance, only it's a little smallish. Not *too* small, I think, after all, I'm just a little car, or more accurately, I'm a little woman, toting two little kids in a little car. I think we can fit in this spot 'cause I feel certain we've squeezed into smaller. Only I'm not so good with geometry. If "Angles and How to Use Them while Driving and Parking" were a course, I'd have flunked it. I can parallel park fairly well, but that's 'cause it feels intuitive. Assessing spatial relationships in the brain—not so much.

I try to maneuver the dang little car into the little space, and for some inexplicable reason, I keep hitting the curb. No amount of backing up and pulling forward, while steering the wheel this way or that, seems to be improving things. Effort is to no avail without skill. However, I'm not prepared to let an unfortunate angle thing interfere with today's shopping trip. I just need a few important items like deli turkey for lunches and a truckload of Coconut Bliss (our family's favorite ice-cream substitute) for my love's upcoming birthday party.

If I can't avoid the curb, I'll just pull all the way up on it, in a spirit of "If you can't beat 'em, join 'em." When the time comes, I'll back off it nice 'n' easy on the way out. I've done that before. Not great for the car, no worse than hitting a speed bump while traveling over the 5 mile an hour speed limit, which I have done, inadvertently, on more than one occasion.

I extract Gabriel and Avriana from their car seats and the three of us head for the store. The munchkins head straight for the car carts that every kid I've ever met seems to love, and so commences the usual dance of squishing, sharing, squabbling, and switching places, until after a few minutes, Gabe takes me up on an invitation to join me as my special helper, leaving the fake steering wheel to his little sister, who drives on with vigor.

By the time I walk out of the store with my two little kids, we have five containers of Coconut Bliss, a cactus, honey roasted turkey, and a few other things. Everything fits easily into two bags. I'm wearing a yellow car sticker on my face, from when the checkout lady gave the kids stickers and Avsi insisted that I have one too. Gabe selected the yellow car one on my behalf. "Where shall I put it?" I ask, looking at both of them.

"Right there," says Avsi, pointing definitively to my left cheek.

As the three of us approach our vehicle, our little troop is fairly content. I'm feeling pretty happy and a light breeze blows by, as if to acknowledge that yes life is good and there is much to be thankful for today. The absence of fussiness is a notable attribute of the present, a true gift.

Kids belted in, I turn on the Prius, look over my shoulder, and calmly and slowly press the gas pedal, intending to ease off the curb.

The car moves backward a little and then the car suddenly drops off, almost as if it lost a tire, or something. We are tilting and whatever the car has dropped into it's not the smooth solid feeling of a paved parking lot, or road, or even off-road gravel, like the other times I've had to back off a curb. It's not like that at all.

I try adding some *umph* to the gas pedal. The excellent news is the wheels are still attached to the car. Here's the not-so-great news: Our wheels are spinning in utter futility, spewing out brown mud like a sprinkler system with a bad case of diarrhea.

This isn't exactly what I had in mind.

I step out of the car to have a look and find the wheel profoundly lodged in a puddle on the far side of the curb. The wheel itself has no intention of going anywhere and the puddle looks like it wants to be a large African watering hole when it grows up. It's clear enough I'm not going to get out of this one on my own.

Somehow, the confidence that at the end of the day everyone and everything will be fine in the sense of no one dying, combined with the obvious fact that my car isn't going anywhere without intervention, has me feeling oddly empowered. The line between what I can do and what I can't do is clear, and the path of action is pretty straightforward. First, I need to borrow a phone. Since New Seasons advertises itself as the "Friendliest Store in Town," I'm confident I'll find someone with a phone who is kind enough to let me call Triple A.

I calmly explain what's happening to the kids, and letting them know that we are going to find someone to help us I extract them gently from seats into which I just placed them minutes ago. "We are going to find a nice person who will let us use their phone to call Triple A. Then a tow truck will come and pull our car out of the mud." Gabe and Avsi nod with understanding. Their faces are focused, and I have the feeling that we are in this together.

I'm so happy both little kids are peaceful and in a fine mood. I would totally rather be dealing with a stuck car than a fussy afternoon or a temper tantrum. Everything is fine if everyone is happy, as far as I'm concerned. I hope I'll make it in time to pick up Nika from French, but even if I'm delayed, it's easy enough to look up the school's contact info and let the office know. It's not like they'll give her away if I'm late, and, thank God, she's old enough to get the concept that her mother did something silly and perhaps untimely, but not fatal.

With a small hand in each of my palms, I remind Gabe and Avsi to check if it's safe before crossing the parking lot to ask for help. As we look both ways, a blue van pulls in front of us and stops. We take a step. Out of the blue van steps a fortyish well-built man with dark hair and a salt-and-pepper goatee. He approaches the kids and me, surveying us and the car with its wheel 6 inches into intractable mud. "Are you the ones stuck here?" inquires the man.

"Yes, that's us," I say, almost proudly. It's not that I'm proud of my parking skills or the situation I find myself in, it's just that I'm proud that I'm having this attitude of "Life's an adventure," and I'm not having a freak-out, which totally could have been an option.

The man with the salt-and-pepper goatee says he thinks he can get my car out. The guy looks really energized and focused, like he's happy to have a chance to do something heroic and helpful. He says something about finding a piece of wood.

Glancing down at my little ones to see what they're making of all this, I notice that while Avsi is looking completely chill and objectively curious, her brother is looking concerned. Upon closer examination, I see that his face is contorting into a quivering squished-up look, like the kind he gets when held-back tears are about to come flooding out of his large almond-shaped eyes.

"How will we get home, Mommy?" Gabe asks, trembling.

Of all my kids, Gabe is the homebody. The helper. The one who likes predictability and a plan. Of the three kids, he is the only one who was *planned* in the first place. We figured Christmas break was the closest thing Ko would get to paternity leave during med school, so that's the window we shot for, and surprisingly, we nailed it. Gabe was born December 18th, two days after my love finished fall term. I wonder if his planned-to-the-week birth contributes to his longing for structure, in contrast to my unplanned daughters, who follow their inclinations wherever their free spirits seem to lead at any given second.

I smooth my little son's soft light-brown hair and wipe the tear droplets from his silky cheek. Squatting on the curb, I reassure him that we will have no problem getting home:

"Either this nice man will help our car get unstuck or we will call Triple A and they will use a tow truck to pull our car out of the mud. Either way, we will be able to drive it home. In the very worst case scenario, we can always call a taxi, or Daddy can come and get us when he gets off of work."

Gabe listens attentively. "So, somehow we will be able to get home, right Mommy?"

"Yes, sweetheart. That's exactly right."

I'm thinking it's gonna be Triple A, but I don't want to steal Mr. Goatee's enthusiasm or put a damper on heroism as a general rule of thumb. God only knows we need more people acting on the heroic impulse to help others.

When I look up from wiping my son's tears, and checking in with Avriana, who remains totally unfazed, I notice a whole entourage of people streaming toward us and our stuck car. Young men and women in uniform (New Season's employees wear bright blue smocks) and everyday Portlanders, old and young, have gathered to join the cause of our stuck-in-the-mud car. In my entire life, I have never had so many people flock to help me for any reason, at any time, ever.

I'm stunned, grateful, and amused. I smile from the inside out.

A group of blue-smocked young adults gather to brainstorm. The cohort is comprised of several guys and one girl, who grins at me and offhandedly boasts that she is the buffest of them all. I overhear them discussing the use of cardboard, firewood, car mechanics, and strategic angles.

A few men of strikingly diverse ages and fitness levels have a try at pushing the car with the pure brute strength of their testosterone-infused bodies. As one slightly cocky-looking guy is giving it his best unsuccessful shot at unearthing my Prius, an onlooker comments, "His eyes were bigger than his muscles." You have to laugh at well-intentioned men in action.

Speaking of being laughed at, I hear a taunting voice addressing itself to me. It's one of the guys who has been discussing the situation intelligently with the other big kids in blue smocks. This fellow is someone who knows how to think in angles and who clearly has the capacity to pass "Geometry for Drivers" if it were a course one could take. Unlike me, this guy also probably would pass "How to Not Beat Up Your Car while Parking" with flying colors. Right now he's staring at the side mirror I snapped off on a post backing out of our building's parking garage when I was in a rush to pick up the kids from preschool one day after an argument with my love.

"Where did you get your license, Oregon or New Jersey?"

"Both," I say, a little embarrassed.

"Are you sure it's not a fake?" says Mr. Smarty Angles in his snappy blue smock.

Mr. Smarty Angles walks around to the other side of my car. Looking at some chalky scratches, he laughs a belly laugh of disbelief.

"How'd you do this?"

"I did that in the parking garage too. On a post."

This fellow clearly thinks I'm an idiot. I could try to explain that our urban parking situation is really tight, but that wouldn't make a dent in his opinion. If I'm telling the truth, which I try to do, when it comes to posts and curbs, I'm a true idiot. It doesn't much matter whether I go by foot or by vehicle. I walk into posts, drive up against them, hit curbs while cruising, and trip over them while strolling. In college I was known for getting lost in the dining hall and bumping into things. Everyone has their talents, and one of mine appears to be giving others something to laugh at, as opposed to with, or anything like "with" that could be considered dignified.

Inside me, an urge is arising to feel a little smart. Cardboard has been inserted strategically under my tire, along with a stick of wood, by people who can think in angles. Someone is in the driver's seat of my car, trying to turn it on. He is not having success. Here it is—my moment to feel truly intelligent!

I peek my head in the window and calmly state, "You don't need to insert the key—the car senses it."

I never pay extra money for car toys, but the fact that our Prius came with this feature does tickle me. It's awfully fun to have a car that is arguably smarter than you are, at least on certain days, like today, for example.

A sarcastic comeback emanates from the driver's seat of my vehicle:

"Ooh, fancy. Round here we use keys."

"You have to have your foot on the brake when you turn it on," I say.

The car is still in off-mode. I walk over, and through the rolled-down window, I press the power button. The dashboard lights up like New York City and I smile.

"I may not be able to park, but at least I can turn on the car," I say in a lame, but fun attempt to reclaim a little self-respect.

At last the time has come to test the collective power of the heroic men and women present. I usher Gabe and Avsi away from the area and out of the line of mud spray soon to come. Then the man with the salt-and-pepper goatee nods to me, puts the Prius in reverse, and revs the engine.

A crowd holds its breath, watching. Oh, oh, YES! There is movement, the wheel is moving, it's up on the curb, it's coming out of the mud! I hear someone yell, "Gun it!" I can feel the excitement build, and then the happy exhale of us all as the car finally crests over the edge and lands without injury within the white lines of a normal little parking spot.

"Wahoo!" I scream like a cheerleader, jumping up and down, still holding hands with Gabe and Avsi. Elation and relief well up into THANK YOU.

I look around at all these strangers. People whose names I don't even know who took the time to help the idiot owner of a beat-up Prius and her kids get the car out of the mud. People with their own lives took time to help *us*. And not because they had to or 'cause community service looks good on applications—human beings helped us because they *wanted to*.

Sure I could have told the folks who wanted to help, "Forget it, lemme call Triple A, it's fine." It might have even been less risky to the muddy underbelly of my car to do it that way. This way was a trillion times more terrifying and terrific.

Lucky me. I got humanity to come together, heroically. I got to feel like part of a freakin' community, even if I was the community idiot.

Of course, being a conscientious mom, it's my ardent wish to communicate the lessons of this afternoon to my young children. As I'm leading them back toward our salvaged little car, I say, "Did you see that, guys? Did you see how everyone helped us? Did you see how everyone worked together as a ... " I am about to say "team," when I feel my foot plunge into a large, murky puddle that looks like it wants to be an African watering hole when it grows up.

As muddy water infiltrates my week-old sneakers, I smile at my kids and finish my thought. "Team. Everyone worked as a team."

Gabe is laughing. "Mommy, your foot got in the same mud that our car was in!"

While my foot marinates in the same muddy waters out of which our car escaped, I carefully pull out of New Season's parking lot and wait until we are cruising to chat more about helping others, working as a team, and feeling thankful for caring, kind people. The kids totally get it.

Gabe exclaims, "Those people helped us and they were so nice!"

Avsi adds, "And they were wearing blue shirts ... and they were helping!"

"And remember the guys put wood under our tire?" Gabe pipes up again.

"I do Gabe," I chime back. "That was so cool!"

Avsi sums it up for everyone: "And, and they were all working together, and they were helping because they like to help, and, and well, uh, they helped us, so they were good boys, and there was one girl and she was good too."

"So Mommy, now we can drive away in our Prius to get Nika and then we can go home!" Gabe says, transitioning us to the next leg of our journey.

Life is filled with muddy waters. Today when I was literally stuck in the mud, I met three friends: grace, humor, and kindness. As a result, I find myself washed in a sea of gratitude and little floating bubbles of joy.

35

Loving Gabe

February 1st, 2010

I let the preschool door close behind me and wave goodbye to Avriana. She waves back, standing in her poop-stained undies, which Erin is helping her out of, while I literally skip out the door to a little boy who is waiting happily in the car. From 10 feet away, I can see Gabe's mile-wide grin and his sparkling brown eyes.

Plaintively he has been whining, fussing, begging, and all-out pleading for a day off from school to hang out with me ever since his older sister had one a few weeks ago. On top of that, he has had an acute case of clingy-itis, which medically translated, means inflammation of the clinginess, when sitters come to our house.

Internship has been hard on Gabe, who's always had a strong connection with his dad, and an ever-changing, family-unfriendly schedule takes its toll on the best of us, including little boys. When I go out to see a client, otherwise work, take a walk, savor happy-hour snacks with a friend, or enjoy a hot beverage in quietude, even an hour of separation seems to exacerbate our little guy's longing for family togetherness. Sometimes Gabe expresses his feelings of helpless dismay by telling me I'm not the right mama for him, or that he doesn't like me, so will I please stay with him all the time?

The other day Gabe said it most to the point: "I want Mommy to not go out and to be with me all the time … actually, I want Mommy *and* Daddy to stay with me every day. I miss Daddy when he's on-call, so I don't want Daddy to be on-call anymore, ever again. Okay? Can we do that please, PLEASE, can we make that happen?"

Understandable sentiments.

Earlier in the week, Gabe got to pick Thursday or Friday for his mother-son date. He picked Friday, which is today.

Pulling away from the preschool, we head down a road that leads to the road with a fork. I offer my sweet, delighted little Gabe the option of going home or going to the zoo. He opts for the zoo, which is a tiny bit unexpected coming from the official homebody of our family. Gabe has always loved to be home more than either of my daughters. It's sort of fun to be surprised by my son. It's true what they say, life is full of surprises.

I have noticed contrary to popular opinion that people do change when we let them be somebody different today than they were yesterday. Yesterday Gabe was a homebody; today Gabe is hungry for a mother-son adventure. So am I. For a directionally impaired person, I am quite impressed with myself for finding the zoo without incident or wrong turn. Perhaps it has nothing to do with improvements in my traveling savvy and instead is simply a facet of the day's unspeakable grace.

Lifting my son from his booster seat, I hold him like a living treasure, which is what he is, what he has always been, even when I have been too inundated with stress or lost in a land of mental preoccupation to sense it fully.

It's the first time in Gabe's whole life that the two of us have an unhurried block of time intentionally devoted only to one thing: being with each other, free of any other concerns or things on our to-do list. But more significantly, it feels like the first time I'm totally *with* him. There is a time for everything, and this is *our* time. TGIF. Thank God it's Friday and I'm with my little boy. For those who, for whatever reason, missed out on infant bliss or angelic baby bonding, it's never too late. It's never too late, thank God, which I do, as joy washes over me. It's the kind of joy that springs from gratitude. The kind that will make you cry if you let it.

I carry Gabe tenderly across the parking lot in the fresh air. I have more than enough sunshine inside to compensate for the cloudy day. I can feel blissful energy flowing like the force of love itself between Gabe and me. It is a holy and wonder-filled feeling, like divine dancing in our cells and in the space between us, which is no distance at all. Never have two people been so happy walking across a parking lot. Each step I take is punctuated by the click-thud of my high-heel boots, which in retrospect may have been a poor choice in shoes. No matter, the click-thuds infuse each stride into timeless remembrance.

Our first stop is the bathroom. Even extraordinary days are ordinary days when you have kids. Eating, peeing, pooping, needing to pull a step stool closer to the sink to reach the faucet. Thankfully, the zoo has a kid-height sink so the step stool only has to be dragged a few feet into place. I marvel at the way my son can independently take care of his own bodily functions and the sweet chubbiness of his little hands as he dangles them under the water. I still have to remind him to scrub-a-dub.

Gabe and I try to have our overpriced photo taken in one of those tourist-trap picture booths, because this is one of those days worth carving into a film strip decorated with zebras. But, possibly in an

anti-consumerist move on the part of the Universe, or perhaps because God knows what we experience and internalize in our spirit
is of greater importance than what can be captured in an image, the
photo booth is out of order. We try another one and it too is on the
fritz. It's okay. We are enjoying the present, which truly is a precious gift. I trust that we are both putting this time into our souls,
and even without a visual record, I have a feeling we'll remember
"the day we went to the zoo, just the two of us" for a long time.

Pouring rain pelts us as Gabe and I plot a course through the
showers toward the sea otters. The air is fresh and filled with happiness, even as we go from feeling joyfully chill to feeling joyful,
but chilly. It doesn't matter that by the time we get to Sea Otter
Cove, the two of us are cold and dripping wet, as we head for
someplace to warm up. I think we may have seen one animal. It
doesn't matter.

Once inside the Zoo Café, my sweet son and I share a hot chocolate, poured in two cups. For today at least, that is how I feel, like
we are one being, poured in two cups. Gabe picks out a square table
in the middle of the empty cafeteria, where we sit. With raincoats
quickly removed, we hold hands across the table and chat about
how our hot chocolates are the same, except that his is a little different because it has whipped cream.

Is this the falling in love that I missed when I gave birth in a
mindset so full of fear that I blocked out the bliss of infinity touching flesh before my eyes? I pray that I will always remember the
sweet smell of my little boy's lovely essence, even when cloud nine
meets the dinner table.

Gabe and I meander through the gift shop. He picks out a
mother-son panda set to commemorate our time. We also purchase Putumayo CDs for each of the girls in our family to let them

know we are thinking of them too! After stopping off at the World Forestry Center, a few feet from the zoo, we head back to the car.

On the way to pick up Avriana from preschool, we stop at Diprimi Dulce, an Italian coffee shop in North Portland, where the sign on the wall says, "My idea of a balanced diet is a cookie in each hand." Gabe orders a strawberry steamer; I get a raspberry mocha. And we sip. Every sip is a moment of togetherness. When our last minute is up, Gabe lets me know he has chosen to save some of his steamer for Avsi, because it is pink, and Avsi likes pink.

36

What Is Medicine?

February 1st, 2010

I look at my husband's reflection in the mirror as he shaves with the focus of someone who alternately wants to go slowly enough to avoid nicks and fast enough to avoid an attending's rebuke for lateness. It's his first day of his final eight-week stint on the medicine service for intern year. Medicine service means long hours and weekly 30-hour call, so I don't like it. On the medicine service, my love is gone when normal people are still sleeping. Hubby leaves at 5:30 in the morning, and except for our oldest, who effortlessly sleeps through fire alarms, the kids sense he's gone. If I'm lucky, I've got until 5:40, when that "Where's Daddy?" sense kicks in and everyone is up. Before 6 in the morning, I'm mediating territorial quarrels by admonishing my children with the reminder that they are peacemakers and capable of finding win-win solutions. By 6:10 I'm stirring buckwheat cereal, locating napkins for the inevitable spills (mostly Gabe's, since he is less physically coordinated, more the absentminded professor type), as well as putting out fires when Avsi is set off by a single grain of buckwheat on her pretty dress. She would easily qualify for a starring role in *The Princess and the Pea*. Thankfully, she also has a down-to-earth helpful side. If Gabe is tired of carrying his backpack, Avsi will hoist it on her shoulder, in addition to her own. If I can't find the scissors, Avsi will jump up, locate them efficiently, and hand them to me without judgment. "Here you go, Mom."

The other thing that's tough about intern year, and especially so when my love is on the medicine service, is how arbitrary his homecoming is each day. Why is it not okay for him to arrive at any time within a 4-hour window to start the day, but apparently it's okay for the faculty or senior residents to let him go home at 5 once in a while on a kind whim, and then make him start a complicated admission right at 4:55 on other days, causing him to have to stay until 7 or 8? Let me tell you, it is *not* okay.

It isn't accurate to say that there is a typical day as far as getting home. However, more often than not, my love arrives home either after the kids' bedtime or smack in the throes of it, which from the perspective of my own sanity is worse, because it's like having Elmo or Hannah Montana show up when you're trying, against all odds, to edge your children toward the peaceful plummet off the cliff of consciousness into sleep. The hardest part is the not knowing. Will he arbitrarily get done at 5:40, or will bedlam erupt in the hospital, demanding his loyalty to its resolution, even while our own form of chaos begs for his help at home? Intern year has pointed out to me so many ways in which I'm a control freak, ways I had hidden so well, at least from myself. Up until recently, I really thought of myself as a flexible person. I let my kids wear pajamas to school and day clothes to bed, for example. I'm discovering it's easy to let go of things we don't care about and a heck of a lot harder to be all Zen about things on which we irrationally feel our very lives depend. On some primal level, I guess I feel like my life depends on some-one being able to say when they'll be home, and then be there.

Watching the rhythmic shaving of the razor across my hus-band's gentle face, I begin the countdown. Even though it's just the countdown toward being done with my least-favorite rotation, instead of the countdown toward the conclusion of the indentured servitude we like to call residency, it's a start.

My love and I have tried to find various strategies for navigating between the twin asteroids of the dysfunctional medical system in which he participates and my dysfunctional relationship with expectations and time. Often the asteroids collide, sometimes we evade them, and occasionally we connect with the Source that dissolves them into spacious, wonderful nothing.

We have tried having him stay out until after I've put the kids to bed and had a few minutes of downtime on purpose, regardless of the time he gets off work. Even though that strategy evokes feelings of single motherhood in certain ways, it's an approach that is empowering. *I love you and I can do this without you.* Taking this approach works pretty well, most of the time, except for a few snags: the first of which is that I feel tremendously guilty for depriving my kids of their dad on the evenings he may actually have gotten home in time to tumble with them on the floor and read them a story. Second, deep down I *don't want to do it myself.* I may be able to override them a lot of the time, but I have needs too, and on top of the needs that I defer or deny in order to function on my own with three intense kids, I have an abiding wish, a longing, in fact, for the intimate wholeness of partnership. Pretending you're fine without any help can feel oh-so independent and sexy for a while, and I'll admit, here and there, that little high has been an important short-term fix. In the long run, though, the roots of resentment that such posturing breeds isn't worth it.

For a while, my love and I tried having him tell me an "outside time" at which he promised to be home. A nice thought in theory. Leave yourself a thick buffer and you don't get disappointed. The only problem with that tactic was that we lacked buy-in from the residency program, which violated our "outside time" with the consistency of a Swiss watch. You can imagine the feeling of devastation when you realize that you have absolutely no control and that your husband has opted into a system that devours his good intentions with the ease of a kid wolfing down a bowl of sugary breakfast cereal.

So we find ourselves engaged in a new experiment in operating day to day without expectations one way or the other regarding his dismissal from work and subsequent showing up for the kids and me with a whole range of outcomes. When I'm happy with my work life and the kids have been relatively easygoing, and my hormones are less crazy than they are at certain intervals, the outcome is a sense of inner and outer freedom and an independent-interdependent feeling when we finally meet up that is conducive to play flirtation and unstoppable sexual tension. On the other hand, when the winds of circumstance consort to frustrate my best laid personal and professional plans, the kids penetrate my inmost resources and deplete them with ungodly efficiency, and my hormones have gone south, trying to act like I am fine with whenever my husband gets home is like pretending you are fine while an 8-inch gash in your leg is overflowing with pus. This week the pus isn't overflowing, it's fomenting under the skin, preparing to burst, given time and opportune conditions.

While my husband shaves the last scruffy section of his cheek, I pull out a comb and start threading it through my hair. I turn to my love and ask, "What is medicine?" It's half a genuine philosophical question and partly the rhetorical inquiry of a sarcastic woman who just has had enough.

"Like, is it not medicine if you don't give a person a prescription?"

My love doesn't say anything. He probably isn't sure whether I'm really asking a question or merely venting my sarcastic angst.

I press for a response, as though getting one will help in some way.

"Why not call it 'broad-scope patient care'? That sounds pretty good, doesn't it?"

My husband chuckles. Is he chuckling at my introspective bent toward tweaking ideas with words, or is it the awkward chuckle born of the discrepancy between my hatred of the medicine service and his overall pleasure in the role he plays on this hospital-based rotation? It's hard to tell.

My husband likes the hospital setting because it has its own routine. When rounds occur, what type of charting is expected, procedures for admitting and discharging patients, and a clear-cut situation for most patients—they either get better and go home or they get worse and they die. Either way, you get to make a meaningful difference in the experience of the patient and their family. My love enjoys the stimulation of medically interesting patients and he also appreciates that, in contrast to an office visit, *he* is the one to leave the room, which comes in handy when dealing with patients who are extremely taxing or like to talk your ear off.

Not that I want my kids to be physically incapacitated, but I totally get what my husband likes about being able to simply exit the room of a difficult person without being followed. I think I would like to work in a parenting setting where you get to walk into a room, be fully present with your kids for a while, let them know calmly when you have 5 minutes left, and then leave the room when it feels like the right time to make a fast exit.

Last night, following a day that felt like interval training, with periods of laughter and loving connection, followed by intensive cross-training zones, made more intense by whatever bug I'm fighting, my love and I watched *The Last Holiday,* where Queen Latifah plays a retail worker named Georgia who gets misdiagnosed with a fatal tumor. Believing she has only a few weeks to live, she blows her lifetime of frugality living large, fulfilling the dreams she has documented in her Book of Possibilities. In the course of her own simple objective to live fully for a few weeks before the end of her life, this woman's infectious fearlessness transforms the greediest and grumpiest around her at the Grand Hotel Pupp (pronounced Poop). When it's discovered that the diagnoses resulted from a faulty MRI machine, it's not just Georgia who gets a second chance at life.

I think about the chronic stress of dealing with toddlers and little kids for years on end, when I'm not innately what I'd call "a little kid person." I feel in my element most with people who look and act relatively put together on the outside and have the self-regulatory ability to only shit when it's appropriate. I like people who can follow two-step instructions, who only have tantrums once in a while, preferably in a professional setting where it's encouraged, and who can verbally debrief these experiences using conceptual models and insights.

If I thought my life was ending in a few weeks, I don't imagine I'd want to blow all my money on a world-class hotel. I've been to a few. My extended family on my mother's side (the ones descended from the *Mayflower* Pilgrims) has these meetings every few years at fancy hotels, and I went to a few. Back then they used to be "covered," I'm not sure exactly by whom, but not by me, in any event.

At one of these events, the melti-est chocolate-chip walnut cookies were served in the evening before bed, following live music for swing dancing. The doormen opened the door for me and every other guest as though we were all queens or dignitaries. The assumption at these sorts of places is that you are either an actual somebody or you are somebody with a lot of dough whose butt is going to get thoroughly kissed. You could just as easily trade places with the doorman simply by trading bank accounts or friends. Even then, there's the fact that the door holders and butlers often look kinder and happier than the guests at these hotels. I'm not saying it isn't fun to play in the lap of luxury once a while. I'm just saying, if I had a few weeks to live, I would give anything for one more opportunity to be with my kids. I'd probably be thrilled to get them one more glass of water, imbued with my love for them, or to help them with their pajamas, even when I'm tired and I know they can do it themselves, just because they like it when I'm there with them. I'd be honored. Filled with gratitude and love. I wouldn't waste time on power struggles with my oldest. I'd turn her morning grumpiness into a chance to laugh together, or if that weren't possible, I'd have empathy and I'd just love her unconditionally, understanding that it's tough when you just don't want to do something. I get that, truly I do. It's just that ordinarily I hate dealing with it, to the point where I feel that dealing with it is shortening my life, and that pisses me off. But if my life were already short, I wouldn't care for my own sake. I'd put her first. I'd put every one of them first.

If I were the lady with the misdiagnosed three weeks to live, I'd live here, in my own life. I'd be so happy to get to live and truly occupy the space of my own life, with the people I cherish most in the world. I would just love him. Which reminds me of something. When I was first a parent, every time I saw a happy-looking older person or couple and learned that they had grownup kids, even if I had never met them before, I'd say, "What's your advice?" They all said the same thing: "Love them. Just love them. Enjoy them. Read them one more story." There was wistfulness in their voices. However loving they had been, whatever mistakes had been made, however successful and thriving their children, you could ache with the feeling that if only they could, they would go back in time and love their kids even harder ... or softer.

It's a fact that bridges have fallen on people, earthquakes have erupted out of nowhere, cars with screwed-up computer interfaces have lurched out of control, truncating lives in an instant. If I live like I have no idea if today is my last day or the first day of 100 years more, what would change in me?

I think it's time to look at myself in the mirror, instead of watching my husband shave.

That's the medicine I'm taking today.

37

Carrying a Tent in Heels

March 1, 2010

Certain things in life lend themselves to a natural high, like sky-diving, being introduced to your crush, running a marathon, and the first time you realize that you like the person you're finally becoming. Then there are experiences that offer you the feeling that, having done that, you could probably do pretty much anything. Sailing solo around the world, completing an Iron Man race, and natural childbirth come to mind. You can think of others, I'm sure.

The thing about endeavors that lead to natural highs and the inflation of self-confidence is that they almost always involve three factors that typically deter us from them: risk, pain, and possible humiliation.

Today I'm attempting a feat that involves only the tiniest bit of each: carrying a six-person tent down two flights of REI's metal steps, out the door, across the street, and into the trunk of my Prius. In heels.

The tent is a surprise for my love, whose birthday is today. His mom and I went in on it together.

Since my love will be post-call today, we'll get to celebrate together in the afternoon. This window of time in the A.M. is my opportunity to sneak the tent into the apartment without his nose sniffing it out. Gabe and Avsi are at preschool and I've left Nika home alone for 10 minutes while I pick up the tent, which has already been paid for online.

Until 4 minutes ago, I didn't know pickups at REI were on the second level. Nor did I anticipate that the youngish guy who handed off the tent to me would ask, "Can you get that all right?" in a tone of voice that clearly is making the assumption that I am a buff outdoorsy person who of course can handle it without help.

I'm not the least bit of a buff outdoorsy person. Let's talk about my un-buffness first. I am a tiny person. I am less than 5 feet tall, weigh between 96 and 105, depending on what time of month it is, and have the biceps of a nine-year-old.

As far as outdoorsy is concerned, I like the healing presence of nature, the zing of earth energy and life exploding in full color, the smell of flowers and dirt, the peaceful rootedness of trees, the lush meadows where fawns graze. I like all of this, as long as I don't get more than one or two mosquito bites, as long as all I have to do is a hold a pole here or there while someone else sets everything up, and as long as I don't have to do number two in a hole in the ground.

Yet, here I am, in heels, being handed a tent.

Fortunately, the tent comes in a bag with straps, identical to an enormous backpack. I inhale deeply and sling the tent onto my back, one skinny arm at a time. I take the steps one at a time, too. I constantly tell my kids to be "careful and confident." I channel my own counsel and I happily make it down the two flights of metal steps, out the door, and into the car without losing face and tumbling head over heels. Everything is intact, including my pride, and unexpectedly, there is another feeling too—one that actually seems to be supplanting the pride with something far more effervescent: joy. It's joy in the silliness of carrying a tent in heels, joy in the fact that I did it, the cloud-nine joy of life itself.

When I arrive home, tent in hand, Nika is fine, as expected. Ordinarily she would be at school, but upon waking up today, she asked me for a day to get better from her cold. Since she had no fever, I was tempted to force my daughter to go to school.

Thoughts of trading my precious few hours of silent house space with the freedom to come and go for a morning of inevitable interruptions and the imposition of potentially irritating requests filled me with dreadful trepidation. Yet my little girl's eyes implored me, opening wide, as if displaying her heart. I felt, initially, a compulsion to turn her off, like an annoying alarm. I felt overworked, overwhelmed, and like I didn't feel like giving ground. It felt like "my needs versus your needs," which is how it often feels when human beings live together in a state of interdependence.

Fear is a terrible enemy because it wants to protect you, but 9 times out of 10, raising your defenses signals out to whomever or whatever you are protecting yourself against, and instinctively, your opponent launches an intensified assault. Living out of fear leads to war, because no matter how good your defenses are, they will not hold. You will either be defeated or you will prevail at the cost of your opponent's life, emotional or otherwise. I know there are better ways to operate in relationships. I just can't always think of them, or implement them, and especially if I'm in a certain state of mind, like tired, freaked out, oppressed, or out of control. Much like our international situation.

Outside-the-box, win-win, synergistic solutions just don't emerge out of that kind of brain state, do they? I know my own brain when I'm stressed, and based on that evidence, I think not. When you're scared and stressed shitless, truthfully you're not even safe to drive, much less come up with innovative ways to live together in peace.

Necessity is the mother of invention, but mothers and even world leaders need time to calm down before they can invent much of anything other than creative methods of mass destruction.

I gaze into Nika's eyes, with my hands on the trigger, ready to just make her go to school, screw her feelings about it, and I stop myself from pulling the release. I take a breath and an idea comes instantly.

"I'm going to take a little time to listen to my intuition, and ask God about it. Then I'll let you know what I decide."

"Okay Mama," Nika says. I could tell she was glad to have her feelings thought of, yet anxious about the outcome.

In the sanctuary of my bathroom, struggling to hear the still small whisper of truth, I find instead endless, noisy emotional static. Even so, I muster enough presence to ask myself what decision would be the highest and truest looking back 20 years from now. Her eyes come to the fore in my inner sight. Looking into them, I'd be hard pressed not to regret making her go. I would wish I had let her have a home day. The other thing that crystallizes has to do with motive. If I force her to go, it would be a decision bred in the dark caves of fear, not the furnace of love's high call.

"Well, what did God say?" asks Nika, peering at me expectantly, her face turned upward, with a hopeful expression traced with a hint of concern.

I look her in the eye. I'm going to leap out on a limb and trust that there is a way for us both to be happy.

"What do you think?" I asked.

"Uh ... I can stay home?"

Her mouth stretched into a banana-size smile. I was still a little nervous. Yet it has turned into a lovely morning.

We sit together at the table and make birthday signs for tomorrow's celebration. Nika crafts a poster for her dad that says, "It's your day, not ours."

I write one that says, "It's your birthday. Do whatever you want!" It seems we have a theme. Maybe it's because, as the older females in the family, we intuitively sense that our guy normally puts others first and often dismisses his own wishes.

After hanging up Happy Birthday signs, we move with ease between doing our own thing and overlapping into shared moments. Unexpectedly, we find our peaceful, fun groove with each other, and the thing I thought would be a burden turns out to be a joy. It's easy to say yes to love, once you're cruising.

Nika and I are reading books, side by side, when she turns to me and says to me, her voice so earnest and angelically sweet, "I'm really glad I got to have a home day ... I think I really needed it and I'm already feeling better." I've made plenty of really big mistakes as a parent, but today I did something that left my daughter basking in love's halo.

I kiss her on the head, then tick off a few to-do's on the computer, like following up with clients and looking up some information.

Once my laptop clicks shut, Nika and I snuggle in bed and watch the last half of *Princess Diaries II*. During the long kissing parts, she hides under the blankets. Let's hope it stays that way for a while.

Later in the day, when everyone, including the man, is home in one piece, the five of us chomp on gluten-free pizza, dance to music selected by Pandora Radio, and sing happily off-key as I unveil the ice-cream cake the kids and I made last night. The crust is melted-down gluten-free Oreo-style cookies and the ice cream isn't ice cream: It's a montage of hemp- and coconut-based frozen desserts with essences of mint and chocolate. I can't do a whole lot in the kitchen, but this creation is *yummy*.

Nika, Gabe, Avsi, and I offer cards and wishes, and eventually we incite the guessing game about big gift hiding under lime-green scarf. With help, my love gets it on the fourth try, and at last we unveil the tent, which I carried in heels. I see approval on his face. The present is a winner. More importantly, I can tell the guy we love so much feels loved and happy, even on less than 2 hours of sleep.

For the party finale, we turn on *Here Come the 123s,* by They Might Be Giants. It's a music video for kids that includes mathematical concepts like zero and everything and lots and lots of sevens. They Might Be Giants is my love's favorite group, and everyone in the family loves their kids' stuff. While sock monkeys sing on screen, my love and I snuggle. Gabe and Avsi watch the video, their eyes glued to the screen like a tongue frozen to ice.

Collapsed on the couch, Nika falls fast asleep while the air is filled with more amp than usual.

I guess she really did need a day of rest! I'm glad I made that choice.

38

The On-Call Room

March 16th, 2010

The on-call room of a hospital is wrapped in images of sleep and its opposite, and of course, sex. Early on in internship year, I asked my love if people really did it in the on-call rooms in his residency program. "Not that I have gotten wind of," he said thoughtfully.

"Well, good," I said at the time.

It may be that everyone is either too tired to have sex or too devoted to their partners or a combination of the two. For a few people, it could be their way of living out the moral high ground of a faith commitment. Whatever the matrix of reasons, I take it as a pretty healthy sign when a residency program attracts interns who can keep it zipped when they're on-call, instead of hopping into bed with each other like in a soap opera.

Stories change with the times, and in the early spring of intern year, my love can't truthfully say that he hasn't heard any stories of interns or residents pairing up intimately in on-call rooms.

I get wind of the latest story while hanging out, catching up after a call shift one afternoon. The kids are half-playing, half-fighting, and intermittently including us in their world in various ways, ranging from requesting that we pretend to be dogs, to asking us to look at their drawings, block creations, and couch tricks. In between solicitations for attention, my love says, "Remind me to tell you a funny story later."

I love funny stories. I look forward to hearing them and sharing them with my love at the end of the day. The laughter feels so wonderful and the silliness of life is delightful to witness together. I like puns, cosmic jokes, unexpected facial expressions, and the belly-laughing humor that life offers up in finer form than your average stand-up comedy guy who thinks that adding the F-word to everything he says makes it funny, which is only that case if your crowd is drunk. I think that's why comedy clubs sort of push the alcohol at their events.

Unfortunately, this week's tales from the world of white coats and sick people have left us with weighty thoughts that would surely bring down Mary Poppins' ceiling-side tea party.

Serious stories have been the staple this week: a drug-addict mom who was told if she uses her IV pick line for anything other than the lifesaving antibiotics she has been prescribed, she will be ineligible for continued treatment. If she can't continue treatment, she'll most likely die. Can she "Just say no" for long enough to say "Yes" to her life? I hope so, oh God, I really do.

Another story my love came home with was about a 40-year-old guy who kept passing out, yet refused the medical team's recommendations to admit him as an in-patient because he is uninsured. Another uninsured person who got pissed off at my love on account of the fact that the hospital pharmacy didn't fill all of his suggested prescriptions for free. Like it was my love's fault. My love would have everybody's prescriptions filled for free, if it were up to him.

I think the U.S. is the only advanced nation that lets people suffer and die when they can't afford treatment or medicine. When will our human decency catch up with our entrepreneurial spirit?

With all these weighty stories of lives and systems run amok, I'm tired of it. Forget important issues, I want to hear about someone getting laid. Fortunately, it's my lucky day.

While the kids are happily careening their scooters around the park, my love says, "So you want to hear the story?"

"Well of course I do!"

My love takes a deep breath before starting the story.

"Okay, so I'm standing in the ER with Nichols and I hear him talking on his iPhone to his current significant other, Jasmine, who works in triage. I hear him look furtively around and whisper, So that's great you get off at 4. Yeah. That sounds good. I'll meet you outside the on-call room in 5 minutes.' "

"Oh my gosh," I say, listening, fully rapt in this gossipy tale.

"Yeah, so then Nichols walks over to me and says, 'Page me if you need me. I'm just gonna go say hi to Jasmine for a little while.' And off he goes."

"You shoulda paged him on purpose!" I say, friskily.

"Well, actually I did page him shortly thereafter, but it was legit," says my love.

"Oh really? Did he sound weird?" I inquire like a high-school girl.

"Actually, he did a little. I guess Nichols must trust me though to let me know what he was up to, more or less."

"I guess so," I reply, not sure what to say.

In my mind, the on-call room has lost its innocence. But then again, Nichols probably wasn't the first to make it in the little square box with a hospital bed. He's just the first one I ever heard about, secondhand. Once that call room was a fresh room, with a spanking new coat of paint on the walls. My curious, slightly dirty mind wonders about the first couple to become one writhing body in that on-call room.

Were they in love, or was it just urge fulfillment? Was it an affair, a fling, or a forever thing? I hope, in my heart, that it was love that first messed up that call-room's sheets for some orderly to send off to laundry services. I hope the two of them made it as a couple, that they are still in love, living to happy old age together somewhere out there.

I'll never know, but I wish I did.

39

I Stole the Bathroom Key

March 20th, 2010

I stand in the looking glass, horrified. I'm staring at my face in the mirror, a pair of scissors in hand. The goal, you may wonder? To repair damage from the second-worst haircut ever to surround my little head. The ultimate, first-worst, hair-related incident occurred in the third grade when my mother, bless her well-intentioned soul, inadvertently gave me sideburns. I remember thinking, how could I ever face my friends looking like Leonard Nimoy!

My love and I have been cutting each other's hair since a month or two into the relationship and usually we do a pretty good job, considering we have never purchased a hair-cutting kit or clippers or anything other than the 99-cent pair of all-purpose scissors that sits in our junk drawer. We originally bought that pair from Michael's Crafts.

Last night I knew my hair had taken a turn for the worse when my love stood silently inspecting me with a look of concern. I wonder if that's the look he wears when he tells a patient that clearly there is something wrong with them, but he's still trying to discern a diagnoses. Then my love speaks in a tone of mustered optimism: "The back looks good but the front is looking a little ... Roman."

My bangs looked like an uneven semicircle around my face, with blunt edges ending at the ears.

Looking myself squarely in the face, with 5 minutes to go before I have a new client meeting, I think to myself, I don't look Roman. I look Romulan.

I snip here and there, evening things out somewhat, making the abysmal bangs shrink shorter and shorter in the process. They are close to even, finally, but there is no subtlety to be found in this cut, nor will there be any use attempting to hide the boldness of the do. It is what it is, pure and simple.

The woman I am meeting momentarily is involved in the fashion industry, so the likelihood of her just not thinking much about my hair or noticing it is nil.

I wet my intense bangs and comb them straight down. *Wear it proudly.* I keep repeating that thought mentally to myself, while applying bright red lipstick that is twice as bright as I ordinarily wear on a date. I figure a little extra makeup may make the whole look come off as more intentional.

No more half seconds to hem and haw. Click, click, click go my taupe heeled boots on the wooden sidewalk, till I'm in the café, sitting beside a lovely woman, who is three-months pregnant and lounging in an elegant comfortable black dress.

The new client meeting is fantastic. I'm facing a person who is as clear about how she is on the inside as she is about what she loves to express on the outside through fashion. Come time to end the meeting, the two of us express how great it's been to connect and how fabulous we each think the other person is and so forth. While she didn't compliment my bangs, she doesn't appear fixated on them, thank God. In the process of heading our separate ways for the day, I find myself ineffectively trying to hold onto the remains of my beverage in one hand, while tying my jacket simultaneously. My beverage cup tips and iced chai spreads like a melting glacier on the floor, in front of me, while I watch with helpless horror.

Onto the next thing. There is no place to go but forward, and out the door as quickly as possible.

I pick Gabe and Avsi up from preschool, emerging from my car to find the earlier clouds have parted into a lovely open-skies day. I stretch my arms up and exhale gratefully.

Gabe runs to the little wooden gate with his hugest smile. Avsi comes and gives my leg a love squeeze before trotting off to get in a few more minutes of play on her "horse," which is actually an upside-down, black, plastic watering can.

I get compliments on my hair from another mom. Erin, the preschool teacher, calls them Betty Paige bangs. "I like them," she says, definitively. My friend Lorna mentions a former employer who insisted that she wear "up bangs," which apparently entails cutting the bangs almost up to the scalp. I told Lorna she ought to sue for hair harassment.

At home, Gabe, Avsi, and I watch from the window as Nika walks off the school bus and confidently strides up to Lovejoy Station's main entrance.

"There she is! There's Nika!" the three of us all say excitedly.

The phone rings. It's the new sitter who is coming to watch everyone while I go to a meeting. Gabe, Avsi, and I go out to meet the sitter, who is slightly disoriented in our neighborhood. We run straight into Nika in the hall.

"Hi sweetie!" I say. "How was your day?"

"Pretty good," she says.

I explain that we're going down to meet the new sitter and inquire if she wants to come or go on into the apartment.

"Why are we getting a new sitter?" Nika inquires.

It's not quite the "Oh c'mon Mom, I don't want to have a sitter" tone. Nika's inquiry is more laced with curiosity and a sense of being caught slightly off guard. Our two usual sitters have become quite the institution, forming the most consistent pattern of our constantly evolving lives. One comes every morning except Mondays for an hour or a little longer. The other comes most evenings for an hour or so. These lovely young women together comprise the third and fourth arm that I need for mothering my kids while sustaining my own soul. Since I couldn't generate actual additional arms, I hired them. I have heard there is a saying that what every wife needs is a wife. This is so true, especially for straight women, who are often married to men who fall into three broad categories: partners who will not share equally in domestic duties, because they think it's women's work, if they think of it at all; partners who want to participate fully in the domestic side of things, but cannot due to their career choices; and partners with flexible jobs or none at all, who try to help out equally with their wives, but get yelled at for doing it the wrong way.

What I'm saying is that the best marital advice I can give is to contract out, in whatever creative way you can imagine and afford, whatever aspects of life cause you the most resentment and the least joy. So long as you hire someone with a caring heart, a fully functioning brain, and a clear background check, even if they don't do things exactly how you would, it's worth it. Think about it, if your husband doesn't do it, then either you have to do it or it doesn't get done. If you do it, you're going to resent the crap out of your husband. If it doesn't get done ... I'll let you figure out how that one plays out. If someone else does it, even if they do it wrong (or maybe just differently), you're going to be mad at someone whose bed you don't have to share.

I understand the curiosity and the innocent caught-off-guard tone in Nika's voice. Why is a sitter who we don't know coming at a time we usually don't have a sitter? I explain that our usual wonderful sitters had other commitments during the timeframe of this particular meeting. Nika is very understanding, accepting, and sweet. "Oh," she says, coming closer alongside me, entraining with my steps.

Everything goes fine with initiating the new sitter, who is a kind and lovely person. The kids take well to her. I can tell they like her by the way all three include her: "Come see this!" "Let's play trains!" "Would you like to watch my trick?"

Check. We are good.

I'm off.

The meeting is totally weird: great people with oddly incompatible styles working on a project. It's almost more awkward than when people you don't think are great have trouble collaborating. In any event, it is interesting. *Interesting* is one of those words Nika and I share in our vocabulary of mutual understanding. Expressed properly, it says everything, with a benign and softly conspiratorial whiff of irony.

Once the meeting is through, I'm left with an hour before I'm expected home, so I decide to stop at my favorite Starbucks and order a hot chocolate. I'm off coffee, at least for a little while. Quitting coffee and all its sweet cousins, like Mocha and Frappuccino and Vanilla Latte, is like giving up a good lover who is bad for you. You know breaking up, or at least taking a break, is the right thing to do, but every day you want it, one more time. You feel weak, and pathetic, and you would be willing to add guilt on top of that, for one more cup. You have to work really, really hard to turn on your frontal lobes and make choices that are rationale.

Today, I crank my frontal lobe for all its worth, while I wait for the lady in front of me, who is ordering something with whipped cream on top. By a hair, I choose the high road for today. I can always choose the low road tomorrow, or maybe choosing the higher way will internalize itself, getting into my blood like an intravenous solution.

I dig out a book, a blank pad, and a pen. I write. Forty minutes later, I have to pee. They have this new thing at most of coffee shops downtown where you have to ask for the key because too many people were using the facilities for drug use. It sucks for the rest of us who just want to make yellow water and go home. It's even worse if you need the bathroom for number two. Once you ask someone at the counter for the key, you wonder if they are thinking about the long crap you just took when you emerge after longer than the usual amount of time it takes to pee. In all likelihood, they are thinking about the macchiato they are preparing, or about whether to get pizza or Chinese takeout after work. They also might be thinking about a film they just saw, or whether or not to get another tattoo, or about their sex life, or lack thereof. They might even be thinking about Goethe or their grandfather or about getting their degree, but there is a tiny chance they might be thinking about whether a certain customer, which could be you, just took a really nasty shit. And that possibility is unnerving.

Today I just want to make yellow water and go home, so when my bladder is too full to hold it for any meaningful additional time I ask the barista for a key. A middle-age man with a graying ponytail is listening in from a small table nearby and chimes in, "See how nicely she asked?"

"Well, I don't let just anyone use the bathroom," says the barista in the kind of tone one would use with a four-year-old or a fourteen-year-old who is about to be given a special conditional privilege. I personally had no idea that the right to pee doesn't exist. Thanks to druggies, it has become a privilege.

The barista goes on: "I say no to people all the time if they look like the kind of folks who might use the bathroom for shenanigans."

"Thank you for not suspecting me of being the kind of person who would use the bathroom for shenanigans," I say as I turn and take quick strides toward the ladies' room.

As I let the door close behind me, I let the black plastic spoon with the key on the end rest in my open pocketbook, since there is no hook to hang it on.

As I do my business, I'm feeling pretty happy about being one of the safe, good, trusted people in the world. When I'm finished making uric acid lemonade, I wash my hands, sling my pocketbook over one shoulder, and walk out the door into the fresh, cooling air of evening.

A full 24 hours later, I look in my pocketbook and see what? A big black plastic spoon, with a Starbuck's key dangling from it.

Lo and behold, I pulled a shenanigan, without ever intending to. I hope no one has busted a bladder on account of my folly. Who knows how many truly good and trustworthy people with a need to pee were turned away because a seemingly innocent, petite brunette used the facilities and made off with the key as casually as the first spring breeze. Worse, what if someone desperately needed to make a bowel movement and developed constipation because they could not follow the dictates of the body's timing?

Once the kids are safely at preschool, I launch project Return Stolen Key to Starbucks. On arriving at 12th and Glisan, I look around to see if anyone recognizes me. It's hard to tell. I wordlessly place the bathroom key on the counter and walk out.

Mission accomplished.

40

The Gate Game

March 21st, 2010

First inklings of daylight shine a pale pinkish light on the over-cast skies outside my window. My love and I have a few minutes to snuggle. Everyone is in the first stages of waking up, prior to full consciousness: little squirms and grunts, an arm or leg flailing, one eye opening, then squeezing tighter, as if to wring the last juices out of sleep.

My love rolls himself off the bed to an upright standing position. He lumbers toward the kitchen and whips up some pancake batter, then wets his hair, combs it quickly, and inserts his feet into work shoes. I alternate between closing my eyes and watching my husband move about with his preparations.

A 30-hour call shift starts in 25 minutes. I hoist myself out of bed and plod toward the kitchen. In between yawns, I ask my love if he has had anything to eat. The pancake batter is sitting in the bowl, ready to turn into pancakes, but there is no time left for the gooey mixture to perform that transformation in time for my love to make his expected arrival time on the Medicine floor for rounds.

My love thought of us, but did he think of what to do about feeding his own energy system? The answer, not surprisingly, is no, he did not. "I'll grab a yogurt or a sandwich from the Physician's Lounge," he says, with a brush of his hand indicating he doesn't want me to worry or sweat it.

Few doctors care adequately for themselves. My love, especially, because he is constantly thinking of others first. I give him a dorky reminder, while I tickle his armpits. "Hey you know, like remember the oxygen mask ... like how you're supposed to put it on yourself first before assisting other passengers?" My love chuckles. "Yes Alicia." It's an honest, yet noncommittal response. Typical.

I surreptitiously fill Avsi's new dinosaur thermos with a high-end liquid meal from Univera and hand it to him. We kiss several times, wish each other a great day, and segue into our completely different weekend experiences.

My weekend will entail an intensive course in learning to be fully present, flexible, and engaged with whatever is happening in front of me ... which, now that I write this, probably is the same thing required of my love. I guess we're on different tracks of the same path.

It's just that my immediate tasks involve flipping pancakes while addressing multiple simultaneous requests for things like books to be read, and undies that someone needs help pulling down, or up, while my love's work entails flipping charts while addressing multiple simultaneous medicines that a patient needs help getting on or off. I am likely to be invited to participate in an imaginary world involving fairies named Sparkle Splash and Flying Flower, and a boy fairy named Tom, while my love is more likely to be invited to a family meeting to discuss whether to take a patient off a ventilator.

With my love off to his day, I turn my focus to scooping up batter and plopping it gently in the frying pan. Avsi puts one of her pancakes in a bowl that is one-third of the way filled with hemp milk leftover from an early-morning granola snack. "It looks like a poop, Mom."

Everyone likes the pancakes, in spite of the one that looks like a poop floating around in a green ceramic toilet bowl filled with milky water. The kids seem in a happy, easygoing mood. When this happens, I'm often caught off guard.

Nika, Gabe, Avriana, and I enjoy a short jaunt to Tanner Springs. The kids bring their scooters and want to play the Gate Game, which my love invented. The Gate Game emerged from a tradition of the kids going out with Dad to Whole Foods. The four of them got such a kick out of the automated voice that says, "Please insert Whole Foods validated ticket," that they turned it into a game.

In the game, the parent or parents, if there are two available, forms a gate, and as the kids scoot up to the gate, the parent(s) have to say: "Please insert Whole Foods validated ticket."

Sometimes a "ticket" is inserted in the form of a high five. Other times the kids flaunt their frisky selves, scooting off squealing, "I didn't insert the Whole Foods validated ticket!" This, in turn, warrants a tickle arrest, or possibly a raspberry fart on the belly.

So even without our main man, we have a ton of fun playing the Gate Game, which the kids could play all day. When I have grown tired of being a gate, I suggest a lap around the park. Avsi and I have a blast jumping off one of the low walls and climbing the little ladder and doing it again. Leaping off a miniature cliff like that feels like flying for a second or two. I may be the only mom in town who leaps in the park, arms outstretched like a bird. Others may be out there; I just haven't met them yet.

Next stop: Title Wave Used Bookstore sale, a 10-minute drive from home. Each kid walks away with a new book and a happy face—all for a grand whopping total of $1.75. Although the children are happy, they are also increasingly hungry, and there is a unanimous request for a trip to Bleuet Organic Yogurt, our favorite FY place, located on NW 23rd Street.

The cool thing about Bleuet is you can get soup, and then you can get frozen yogurt. It is a cheap, painlessly nutritious, and highly delicious way to enjoy an afternoon. We savor our potato leek soup and each other's company at the circular white table in the center of Bleuet. Between sips of broth, we play "I one you, I two you, I three you ... I EIGHT you!" Then a leisurely game of hangman ensues. It seems like Nika is a tiny bit off her center, yet still overall loving, engaged, and flexible, when I point her in a direction, such as "Wait," "Include," etc. Once everyone is connected and included, our simple games are so much fun. Who knew it could be so wonderful to hang out together on a lazy Saturday?

One of our usual sitters comes for 2 hours in the afternoon. Gabe is desperately sad that I'm leaving. He wants more than 14 kisses. I give him 21 Kissing Hands, on the front and back sides of his little hands. Avriana declines a hug, and then decides at the last minute to come over for a kiss. But just a kiss. Nika and I share a love squeeze and I'm out the door.

A few minutes later, I'm sitting between two trees on a trail just inside Forest Park. I'm careful not to squish the flowers that are living in that space too. I'm happy to be able to occupy this space between trees, sharing it with these friendly flowers, without harm. I thank them on my way out of the park. As if in reply, a cool breeze ruffles my bangs.

41

Life's Purpose

March 22, 2010

I am sitting in a Starbuck's in Northwest Portland—not the one where I stole the bathroom key—writing my Life Purpose Statement. After at least 50 tries, here it is:

"To facilitate the flourishing of life wherever I am, for whomever I am with, in whatever way is in the highest, for the highest in each one of us."

For the rest of the day, I observe how this freshly identified Life Purpose Statement informs my life, including the way I respond to others and the overall outcome of what happens in the aftermath of my responses. Nika is a little off her center again today, and it's starting to annoy me deeply, since she is sucking a disproportionate amount of attention away from moments I want to share with my other kids. I don't have one kid, I have three, and yet I have one who wants to be the sun around which I orbit, let the other children traverse the universe on their own. It especially irritates me since we're talking about the oldest eclipsing the younger ones, in what seems like an unreasonable black hole of attention craving.

I can feel the heat head toward boiling, as it often has in the past. I take an alternate path. I write a letter to one of my daughter's alter-egos, a Pegasus named Sparkle Splash, who my little girl often inhabits during mother-daughter imaginative play.

Dear Sparkle Splash,

I have a problem. My little girl, who I love, seems to be wanting more attention than I can give her right now. I love her so much and it is frustrating because it seems like no matter how much attention she gets, it is not enough. I want my Nika to be happy and filled up with love, and I also want to be able to have enough energy and time to connect with my other kids too, because I love everyone in the family, with all my heart. Do you have any advice for me?

Sparkle Splash writes back:

I don't know. Maybe you should talk with your daughter about the situation.

When the letter from Sparkle Splash floats into my lap, I'm splat in the middle of Gabe and Avsi's bedtime. Inhaling intentionally, I stand and move toward Nika, who is sitting in a little nest she has created for herself on the floor, wrapped up in blankets and books and stuffed animals.

I sit by Nika's side, thank her for the letter from Sparkle Splash, and let her know that I want to give her my full presence and complete attention. In order to do that, I explain, I need to first attend to Gabe and Avsi's bedtime, and then have one or two minutes to meditate and center myself.

I tell her, "If you want to, you can write your thoughts and feelings out for me to read and for us to talk through when I'm done with Gabe and Avsi. That way, you can help us get a head start so we don't use all our girl time talking about serious stuff."

"Yeah, Mamasu, that sounds great."

I read Peter Rabbit, Counting Kisses, and Kittycat Lullabye to the little ones, and snuggle them in their bed, until their small bodies rise and fall with the gentle rhythms of sleep. I say a little prayer over them and tiptoe out to the living room to check my "mail." Our family mailbox system is comprised of a mini coat rack with little square cubby holes. The coat hanger pegs sit there unused, while we employ the cubby holes for passing notes and storing little things that tend to get lost. Peeking into the cubby hole labeled "Mom and Dad," I find a note from Nika that says:

Dear Mamasua,

I am wanting attention all day because Dorothy in the Wizard of Oz book goes through an earthquake so I'm always like this if something bad happens in a book like an earthquake I wonder what if there's an earthquake in Oregon and I die so I want to be very near Mamasua/ Cocoabean.

Love,

Nikasua

Well, I hug that girl, and she hugs me tight back, and we settle into a snuggled position on her bed. I mention that while probably there isn't going to be earthquake in Oregon anytime soon, everybody's body dies sooner or later, but the good news is that her spirit is eternal and cannot be harmed. I tell her that people find the ones they love in the place where God is, or in a new life.

175

My oldest girl turns to my enormous anxious eyes and says, "I know everyone dies. I just don't want to die in something horrible like a storm."

"Well, my sweet Nikasu," I say, "I think it's highly likely that we'll both live to a very old age and we'll get to be wrinkly, happy old raisins."

I continue: "Now some parents would probably just say, 'Oh well, don't worry sweetie, I'm sure there won't be an earthquake here—that only happens in California.' But I want you to know, sweet Nika, that nothing can harm the essence of who you are. You body, your feelings, your thoughts—they can all change and end. But *you—the part of you that is made out of God's love*—it can't be hurt and it is eternal. Even if the absolute worst, most frightening thing happened, like a horrible earthquake, you would be okay. Your ultimate essence would be totally fine. I want you to get that, because when you know that EVEN if the very worst thing that could possibly happen happens, you'll be fine, then you can live a life free of fear."

I'm holding Nika like a baby, even though she is almost as big as I am, and I see tears streaming down her face. At first I think I've made a mistake by telling her so much truth at such a tender age.

"I'm not crying sad tears," says Nika. "I'm crying happy tears because of your words."

42

The Sex Appeal of Objectivity

March 25th, 2010

Typically, in the West, marriage is part love affair, part business arrangement, whether or not we admit it. Heck, the government knows it. When you file your taxes together, you are basically filing as a conjugal corporation. Unless you want to limit your relationship to furtive evenings in a secret alcove, embrace the fact that when it comes to life together, you are flying for business and pleasure. It doesn't have to detract from true love. In some cases, it can even fire things up, like an old-fashioned office romance.

My love and I have one particular business arrangement that is working out fabulously. I provide him with life and career coaching; for his part, he fixes and soothes my back with his osteopathic magic.

It's a little unorthodox, but that's half the fun of it.

When I sit down for a coaching session with my husband, he isn't primarily my husband, though of course the underlying truth of our connection is on the table. When I put on my coach's hat with my husband, I'm at least 90 percent professional. For the hour that my love is first and foremost my client, my sole intention is his highest best interest. I follow his agenda and let mine have a rest.

In the free and open space of objectivity, I hear what's important to my love: what he's thinking about, his dreams, struggles, and goals; his feelings, priorities, and processes of thought—things I don't often get to be privy to, at least to such a full extent, in our everyday lives. In the space of coaching, we are taken out of ordinary time, away from the vested interests that sometimes oppose each other and inhibit communication. In different roles, without our wills up to bat, a fresh dynamic emerges. It's one where a feeling of safety, purposefulness, and exploration thrive. It's nice to put aside my personal feelings about internship and how it inevitably shapes the practical form of our partnership in a lopsided fashion. It's like a burden lifted off from me—one I can't free myself from in normal time.

For my love's part, he feels the relief of sharing openly, free of worry over my personal feelings about internship's impact turning to a personal attack. He doesn't have to cower from the feeling that that the intensity of my rage toward "the system" is paramount to a lack of support for who he is and what his path demands. In that space held by professionalism, something holy happens: It's called intimacy.

In coaching, there is a term called "dancing in the moment." It means being intuitively playful and playing off each other in a way that services the client's highest interest. My love and I enjoy dancing in the moment, without touching. The details of our lives and roles sit in the background while we focus, connect, and play in a field of professionalism. It's the ultimate lesson in not taking it personally. By taking myself temporarily out of the equation, I enjoy every woman's dream of a partner who shares intimately, fully, and vulnerably from his inner being, and my love benefits from every man's longing for unconditional support from the woman he adores.

When our coaching session is over, I get a high-quality osteopathic treatment that does wonders for a spine, neck, and sacrum.

We both get to taste each other's professional talents and benefit from them. It's a win/win.

But the really juicy fruit comes when our professionalism is over and we are introduced to each other as life partners as if for the first time. An electricity born of understanding and admiration elicits a response in us that could make the air quiver.

43

Losing Babysitters and Other Signs of Spring

April 1st, 2010

I may have mentioned earlier that my wonderful sitters are like the extra limbs I need but can't grow from my own body, so when my two part-time nannies give notice within 24 hours of each other, I think it must be an April fool's joke played on me by God.

Ha-ha-ha, so funny, God, they aren't really both going to quit and get "real" jobs simultaneously. And God laughs back. "Oh no, it's true."

Why does cosmic humor so often entail upheaval of everything that gives us security? Probably because we'd prefer to stagnate or suffocate in our own little nests of safe familiarity than learn to fly. I heard the other day that mother eagles destroy the nest if their eaglets won't leap off into thin air. It makes sense, but dang, being forced to leap into free fall, you wonder if your wings will hold, and whether you'll find an air current to ride to soaring heights, or if instead you'll plunge straight down into a pile of bloody feathered mess. Every eaglet has these fears, I imagine, including the one typing away here.

Spring is the ultimate time of old forms dissolving into fresh life, like the last of fall's leaves fertilizing this year's flowers, or the mother eagle destroying her offspring's safe haven that has de-volved from a lifeline into an obstruction to life's flourishing.

I know April 1st isn't the official first day of spring, but it seems like it, in a way. It's a day of reckoning, establishing for us that the time of incubation is over, letting old structures dissolve, and trust-ing that the wings I've practiced flapping around will work, and that, somehow, I will find a fresh air current to mount me up into the sky.

Of course, when old structures dissolving looks like your two primary babysitters, who make your entire life a little bit sane, giv-ing you notice at a time when it seems like your whole life is fraying at the seams, it just seems unfair. I wonder if eaglets ever whine to their mothers that it's a bad time to learn how to fly.

Even when what is happening is uncomfortable, there is com-fort in feeling like it's discomfort with a purpose. When untimely things happen in a synchronous way, you can bet the Divine has something to do with it. There is a Greek word, *Kairos,* which means "God's inspired timing." It has nothing to do with our convenience, yet you can sense in it something that energizes you because it's about the larger sweeping scope of life, and you get to play a little amazing part in it.

One of the ways I connect with the whispering intervening of God's hand in the timing of life's events is by observing synchronic-ity. Surely there is some sort of synchronicity of my sitters quitting almost simultaneously. Even in the face of feeling a bit overwhelmed, sensing a higher purpose in the unfolding changes lifts me, leaving me with mingled emotions of helplessness and optimism.

For five or six months, the nest I created around my life was well insulated and wonderfully keeping me safe so I could thrive. The sitters who are quitting came four days a week, for an hour or so in the morning and evening each, giving me an opportunity to take a breath at the beginning of the day, and exhale toward its close. I put into their trusted hands two notable jobs that I found insane: waking the eldest child from her virtually comatose sleep in time for school, and helping the little ones select and don outfits. Even the sitters sometimes couldn't pull it off, and once or twice Avriana rode to preschool wrapped in a white towel. Still, letting someone else handle the incessant pickiness and multiple meltdowns freed me to feel a little more human and to be a more present mom during the hours when I was with them. Having the sitters freed me to spend a lot more time celebrating and honoring my kids instead of wishing away their childhoods with every bit of urgency as Dorothy wishing herself out of Oz.

The fact that my sitters cleaned up after our breakfast and supper brought untold relief and joy, along with a little chunk of time to escape, either on my own or with my love if he happened to get off work in time to rendezvous for a snack or a drink at one of our local establishments. More often than not, my guy finished up in time to at least sit outside in one of the parks close to our home for a few minutes, or sip something in a café for a few minutes, giving us a few inches of intimate buffering against the constant demands of an intense internship, intense kids, and the challenges of starting a career, and a life for that matter, from scratch in a new place.

For a while, the structure I set up worked like a magic pill. I had a fairly balanced life, with enough opportunity for connecting with the kids, creating the beginnings of my own career, spending time with my life partner, and once in a while, having coffee or tea with friend. My structure with the sitters was a safe zone in the otherwise chaotic circumstances of motherhood, internship, and entrepreneurship.

Unfortunately, or perhaps serendipitously, lately the security of my life has been dissolving. As if piece by piece, the life I have worked so hard to build appears to be falling apart on purpose, like someone is destroying my nest or something. Intuition tells me I'm getting kicked out of my safety zone. To the other parts of me, it just seems like everything is falling apart, while I watch.

My love has seemed perpetually stuck at work, for one. At best, this pattern is discouraging. At worst, it's toxic to intimacy. And somewhere in the middle, it just pisses me off, sometimes at the situation, sometimes at him for picking this career, called to it by a higher power or not. I just get selfish sometimes, damn it, and I think, "You *chose* this. It's your fault." Have you ever felt that way?

It's one thing to flex. It's another to feel perpetually left hanging. Then there's the fact that the kids are falling apart too. Gabe has been increasingly off-kilter and upset when I leave for work or to simply "be" for a little while. It's as though every time I depart, even for an hour or two, it's as though his sense of loss over Daddy being gone so much is compounded into this stuck, fussy place inside him. Avsi recently got on the Mommy bandwagon too, and out of the blue started missing me more urgently and frequently. When Avsi gets clingy, wrapping herself around you like seaweed around sushi rice, you know it's a serious longing inside her. Ordinarily, she's off in a flash. Just try to get a hug after dropping her off at pre-school, or on your way out the door. Usually she just won't give you the time of day, not because she isn't affectionate, but because she is a busy person, with a lot on her agenda, like pushing her baby in the stroller or playing "princess," instructing her sister and brother on how to play "horses," or telling her classmates how to get the most flavor out of their vegetables. Lately, it's been seaweed on sushi rice, and separation is heartbreaking.

Meanwhile, several career-related projects flopped on their faces after a lot of hard work. I keep reminding myself how many tries it took to invent the light bulb. But gosh, you know, I don't need to invent anything—I just want to help people live as they are created to live. I have a few wonderful clients, and it's a delight to share in their journey. At the same time, my practice hasn't seemed to launch itself to the point of reaching the tipping point of providing a meaningful supplement to our family's income, which is frustrating. It seems like most people in my circle of influence are either too busy or too broke to take time out to invest in their own potential.

Then there's my relationship. You know, the intimate one, with my love. Old issues we used to more or less effectively cover up with bandages and tape started oozing. Unhealed wounds insisted on casting off our habitual, periodic re-taping. Ancient coping strategies stopped cutting it.

In the course of things, as old wrappings were discarded, my love and I saw that some unresolved pieces of our relationship had been suffering from a long sustained infection. The pus was really yucky. Yet the essence of our connection seemed to be calling out: "Hey, over here. I'd like to heal, but this infected wound demands some serious cleaning out, or it's gonna cost you."

Conscious enough to get the message, but struggling to know how to heal, we fought a lot. Then, over a week or two, spring finished its work. Our nest—the assumptions we had been living with about ourselves, our choices, and our relationship, and our expectations of one another—was collaboratively dismantled. It was as if we were both the mother eagle, intuiting that our relationship could not achieve the soaring heights of its destiny without the destruction of its outdated nest.

When there was one twig left, we leapt into free fall. In that act of leaping, my love and I found out something wonderful: The two of us are in love with each other. That is the abiding truth when everything else is stripped away. Yes, we're imperfect. Yes, we've screwed up, been immature, and wish we could go back and change the details of our history. But the fundamental fact of our love is like the sky, and we wouldn't trade it for an easier path. That truth sets us free to let go of the past by changing our relationship with it. This might sound kind of weird, but I think you can come within an inch of changing the past by means of an intentional "Take Two." When my love and I shared the sense of wishing we could have been the people we are now back then, when the genesis of our emotional infection took root, we decided to take our current selves back to those situations and do something about it, by reenacting two pivotal conversations that shaped our dynamic for endless rounds of the same of shit, thereby shifting the energetics of those events. It helped that we both have a secret flare for acting, and for being willing to get quirky for a good cause, like our intimate connection. Let me tell you, I have never felt so transformed from the inside out within minutes. It felt like time traveling, in a way. And when we came back to the present, everything was a little bit different, as though our Take Two altered both our internal sensibilities, along with the fabric of our interactive style with each other. Better than therapy or drugs, that trip blessed us with a fresh feeling of joyful ownership surrounding our choice to share life together in this crazy time of internship.

Old structures dissolve, trusted sitters move forward with their lives, infections heal, eaglets learn to fly, and two lovers in Portland decide that today, April 1st, is the perfect time for a wedding. It's the fourth incarnation of our marriage, so far.

My love and I hurry out the door and across the street to Lovejoy Bakers, where we scribble fresh vows on paper napkins.

Our intentions and promises flow out of fresh insights, forgiveness for ourselves and for the other for past hurts, as well as from the joy we're touching in the core of body and being, where we know in every cellular vibration and soulful resonance that our love is for eternity, whatever arises to support us and force us to fly higher as life unfolds. We affirm our confidence that even when the path is invisible, or the terrain seems impossible, there is a way, beyond willpower and rational understanding, for us to flourish in our callings as individuals, as well as be true to our love for each other and our calling as an intimate twosome. We celebrate each life and our life: two yet one yet two.

With our intentions and promises, my love and I run, holding hands, to our wedding for two, yet one, on the grass steps of Tanner Springs.

"I do."

"I do."

With the lightness of wonder, two sets of lips touch softly. Above us, a bird soars in spirals, higher and higher, as we dash in different directions to accomplish the day's tasks.

44

The Big Three

April 5th, 2010

Tomorrow my last little girl is turning three. It is a huge occasion, not because we have a gigantic party planned, which we don't. I have taped a handmade birthday sign to a chair, made her a card with stickers and pink marker, and muffins are cooking in the oven. I'll swing by New Seasons later, while she is at preschool, to snag a gluten-free chocolate cake mix and white frosting.

In between working from home and picking up from preschool, I'll wrap her present, which is a set of Safari animals and shrubbery that supposedly stick to the bathtub. Then I'll unpack the present out of its ginormous box to reveal a life-size giraffe, which I ordered partly because she likes giraffes, and often pretends that she is the baby giraffe and I am the mama one. The other part of the reason I told Amazon to charge my card and send a huge giraffe to my home is because I always wanted a life-size plush animal as a child, and now I'm unabashedly projecting onto my kid. At least I'm clear about the situation.

My love will be home from night float in the afternoon, in time to see a large tall shape in our living room, shrouded in a silk scarf. We'll have a fun, basic family party—nothing huge or fancy.

Avriana turning three is an important milestone for a number of reasons. First, it marks her survival beyond what early childhood experts like to call the most formative years. The subtext of what the experts really mean is that in addition to physically surviving the first precarious years of life, a child who turns three has been shaped. In sum, a three-year-old has passed through the phase where parents are most acutely prone to either killing the child or letting it become a little dictator. Of course, families, like all institutions, function best when there is collaboration, along with a healthy a balance of power. No one likes to be disempowered. Kids hate it. Parents hate it too. Both the tendency to spoil and the urge to kill spawn from parents feeling disempowered in the face of their child's intensity. The tendency to spoil comes from a sense of defeat. "Yes, fine, you can have whatever you want because I'm too tired to fight. You win." In a way, spoiling a child is giving up on them. On the other hand, the urge to kill comes from a compulsion to win the power struggle at all costs. Hurting or wanting to hurt a child is giving up on ourselves, letting fear, cumulative stress, and desperation storm our castle, desecrate our true intentions, take us over, and pillage what we hold sacred.

Of all my kids, Avsi has been the hardest not to kill, as well as the hardest not to spoil, in part because I see myself in her, sometimes in beautiful ways, sometimes in frightening ways. I never projected onto Nika when she was little, for we were clearly two connected, but very different individuals, from day one. Nika came into the world as a blonde, socially agile extrovert, with a graceful, long body, and a personality like a flitting butterfly attracted to fun with a profound aversion to anything too heavy. Nika is perceptive, caring, and wise. However, she offers her observations and spiritual reflections with the lightness of a girl flicking her hair. I, on the other hand, grew up feeling like a socially confused, introverted brunette, known as "Shorty" from second grade through twelfth. In the fourth grade, my best friend got a supplemental best friend. When I asked why, she said, "Well, Adrian is my *fun* friend and you're, well, I mean you're fun too, but you're my *serious* friend. Like deep, you know?"

I thanked God when Nika was born with a personality all her own. Here was a person distinct enough for me to see, understand, and love as an individual, rather than an approximation or upgrade of myself. Of course, Nika and I have things in common. We are both creative, curious, and empathetic, and we both like to offer our insights and neither of us likes to clean. The thing is, our over-lap emerged with time, after I had already figured out that I was dealing with a unique spirit, who came through me, but was not, in fact, a little version of me.

Gabe came along, and well, assuming you're the mom, it's pretty easy to see that someone who has their thing on the outside instead of the inside is not you. Plus, Gabe has so much of his dad in him: his love of facts, his crystal-clear memory, his acute sense of direction, his observation of form, function, and detail, his practical mindset, longing for structure, helpful spirit, and earnest wish to please the people he loves.

Avriana has a few of her dad's qualities: his face, for one, and also his practicality and sense of precision, his observational acuity, his love of animals, his predilection for nurturing. Otherwise, Avsi is a heck of a lot like her mom: tiny but mighty, passionate, intense, old for her years, competitive, sensitive, artistic, verbal, feisty, affec-tionate, completely un-intimidated by boys twice her size, willful, and unselfconscious about most things, including getting her danc-ing groove on in public. Ironically, because my youngest daughter is so much her own person at such a young age, it's easy to over-identify with her. Which is why, whether she likes it or not, she is getting a life-size giraffe, like I mentioned.

One of the amazing things about Avsi turning three years old is that I haven't killed her. I have come close, more times than I care to I admit. On other occasions, in order to avoid getting to that scary place no parent ever wants to be, I have surrendered to absurd dictates, such as agreeing to pretend to pee on the toilet when I didn't have to. Parenting books say kids' tantrums last 10 to 30 minutes. My kid can go for an hour, or all afternoon, or all night, on and off. It isn't easy or pretty, yet I have come to a hard-won place of fabulous respect for this little person. I freaking admire her. I had no idea one could feel such a sense of equality with someone who is two and a half feet tall. The wonder of it all is that you have to still parent this tiny person who is your equal. What makes it even trickier is the whole projection thing. It can lead you to come down too hard, or to be too lenient. On the other hand, without the ability to put myself in her shoes, and feel like I get where she's coming from, like from the inside out, I'm not sure parenting this princess would be possible. When the parenting books have nothing helpful to say about a situation with Avriana, I can at least reference my own memory of what it was like to feel like an older person, to relate better to adults than to kids my own age, and yet still have to reckon with being a child.

I think the important thing is to balance projection with presence. Presence means being *with,* in a state of un-conditionality. It might feel like empty space, or compassion or holiness. It could feel like nostalgic longing, like you get when a movie or life event makes you realize that there is no good or bad—there's just human beings. Presence could feel like noticing the feeling of having to pee, without actually getting up to use the facilities, or like sitting still and quiet with pizza-born indigestion, just letting it pass. Or it could feel like being the womb of God for someone, or something: yourself for example, or your life's work, or your writhing, screaming child. You know, whatever needs space, yet also needs to feel held.

After several years of practice with Avriana, I'm improving at tapping into presence. I'm still a control freak, but slightly less of the time. I'm a little better than I used to be at letting things be what they are, without feeling the need to stop current reality at all costs. I'm less dangerous, in that sense. I'm also more tuned into what the moment is wanting from me. More space? More holding? Often I intuit at what point Avriana will reach out her arms to be picked up. What an exhale when that finally happens.

When my kids were babies, I was largely cut off from my intuition. I didn't trust the process, or myself. Finding my way toward understanding and intuition is an ongoing trip. I'm happy for the ground covered, for the understanding gained, and the healing that sprinkles itself like fairy dust, deep into the cells of my being. I open up at the apex moment when the time is sweet for things to shift inside, and outside.

Understanding has come with timing's perfection, in unique and wonder-filled ways with each of my kids, and even my spouse. That hard-won understanding is the source of my utmost gratitude, because understanding is intimacy, and intimacy is the celebration of knowing and being known.

Take Avriana: I understand that Avsi needs to do it herself. I understand the value of a river that can flow over rocks and around little islands, while having strong banks. I have learned to put the control in Avriana's hands, as long we are on the same page about where she needs to eventually guide herself. For her part, Avsi understands that after bedtime it is grownup time; therefore, even if she cannot fall asleep, she has to stay in her room. Avriana understands that I understand how hard it is to do that when adults are still up and at it. When I snuggle the blankets around her at bedtime, I tell her about when I was a little girl and I felt like I wanted to be included in what the grownups were doing, because I felt big on the inside. I tell her that I get it. Avriana asks for that story a lot. I truly do understand how dreadful it is to be treated like a child when you are an old soul living in a kid body.

Another reason why Avsi's third birthday is a momentous occasion: She is my last, at least my last biological, baby to officially climb out of babyhood into the clear territory of kid-hood. In spite of the periodic behavioral evidence to the contrary, I have no more babies in the oven, rest assured. Unless I am either the chosen vessel of the next virgin birth, or I am drugged and assaulted, there will be no more occupants in my uterus.

Three weeks after Avriana's arrival, on my love's birthday, he did a very brave and valiant thing: He got a vasectomy, which was performed by the chief of surgery at an East Coast hospital. Sperm, eat your heart out, it's not gonna happen.

That fact is truly relieving, considering that I lost 90 percent of my tooth enamel from puking excessively during my pregnancies. On the other hand, I'm also left with an odd form of emptiness that feels happy, open, and full of a funny, outdated yearning, as if my mind is finally free and my womb is looking around, confused and longing to fulfill once more its intended biological function. It instinctively rejects the idea that life will never come forth from it again. At the same time, my conscious intellect says, "Thank God I'm finished with childbearing." My womb will therefore have to content itself with letting loose its fertility and creative forces in the realm of Spirit and art. The impulse to express life takes its own form in each season with which a woman is blessed.

And speaking of seasons in a woman's life, the other interesting thing about my youngest turning three is that later this year I will turn 30. For both of us, it seems like a year owning selfhood, letting go of outdated behaviors, and engaging the world with a newfound sense of wonder, connection, confidence, and love.

45

Cigarette Break Averts Potential Suicide

April 6, 2010

The fact that humans are not entirely rational beings will not likely surprise you. You have lived with yourself for some time, so you probably have intimate experience with this factoid. If you live with someone else, you really know for sure. And if you work in a hospital as an intern in the ER, you are privy to witness unusual forms of irrationality up close.

True story: There is a schizophrenic guy who's been sleeping with a knife every night for a month contemplating killing himself. The man is a diabetic, but he doesn't like to talk about his diabetes. In fact, discussing his sugar levels was so upsetting that he almost left the hospital AMA (against medical advice). Well, at first, that's why they thought he wanted to leave the hospital. With a little TLC from my husband, it was coaxed out of the patient that what the guy really wanted—why he was about to leave the hospital against medical advice—was because the man wanted a good old-fashioned smoke. Once it was arranged for him to go outside to light up, accompanied by two big buff chaperones, the patient agreed to stay in the hospital.

I guess life is about priorities. For that patient, in that moment, having a smoke was more important than his life and avoiding the anxiety of discussing a medical condition was more pressing than taking steps to increase his health. For my husband, in the role of physician, it was more urgent to secure the patient's voluntary stay at the hospital than to force the issue of his diabetes or his smoking habit. Life is full of tough calls and interesting choices.

In my neighborhood, there is a young woman who works at a coffee shop across the street. In a few weeks, she's moving to Seattle. Not long ago, I saw her smoking outside and asked if she'd thought about quitting. She said she had quit for six months once, but that for some reason it's hard to quit in New York and in Portland. I offered to do a smoking cessation coaching thing for the young woman and her friends. She said she'd talk it over with the others. Although I see the young women frequently, I didn't bring it up again until today, when she told me she's moving really soon. I mentioned it would be great if she took advantage of a free coaching session to help her quit before she heads off to the next leg of her adventure. Of course, setting the agenda for a coaching session is completely un-coach-like, but I hate to see people smoke, especially sweet, kind people I like a whole lot. I'm confident she's probably not going to take me up on the offer anyway.

The young woman smiles. "Actually, I haven't smoked for a while," she responds. Continuing on, she tells me how it happened for her: "I was around my family for a week, and I didn't do it while I was with them. Then I started reading this book about quitting that focuses less on scare tactics and more on why people smoke and kind of dealing with the root causes."

I tell the young woman how happy I am for her and how that approach makes a whole lot of sense. I'm happily relieved. I don't have to coach her on a goal inappropriately set by me. Best of all, this person I care about is caring for herself and taking healthy steps, without my ridiculous interference. Who knows if I influenced her that first day I said something about seriously thinking of quitting or if it would have come about exactly the same without my interference? In all likelihood, she didn't need my help at all. But even if I added a drop to her "quit smoking" bucket, the young woman certainly didn't need my agenda imposed on her.

Interference is a strange thing. When is interference the serendipitous interception of the status quo and when is it us offloading our fix on unsuspecting innocents? If I had it to do over again, I think I'd still ask, "Have you thought of quitting?" Instead of subtly pushing a course of action, like getting her into a cessation group, I'd offer information: "I facilitate coaching groups and if you or any of your friends are ever interested, I can do one for whatever area of focus would be meaningful to you, including smoking cessation if that's on the table." Then I'd smile, lips sealed, and walk away.

So much of life is learning to interfere just a little—then zip it.

46

Un-Schooling in the Shower

April 8th, 2010

It is 9:20 in the morning, and the kids are safe and sound at school. I look up from what I'm doing at the computer when I hear the sound of the shower going. My eyes meet a huge giraffe, that Avriana has named Amy. I smile. It turns out Amy is a hit with everyone in the family. I'm also happy because my love is home after another longish night at the hospital. The schizophrenic guy who needed a smoke eventually agreed to have his sugars monitored, but he continues to refuse insulin. He hears voices saying bad things about him and his father. When my love first got home and I heard this, I thought out loud, "Maybe they could hypnotize him and have the voice say nice, compassionate things." "Yeah," responded my love, "that's good. I like it. Yeah, because that patient's dad had issues and committed suicide, so maybe we could change the voice to say, 'Your father is at peace and he loves you'."

"I like that," I say.

Now I contemplate the sound of the shower pitter-pattering in the bathroom and the fact that I have 40 minutes before I have to be in a teleclass. "I'm coming in," I announce, as I enter the bathroom and strip off everything but my skin.

I hop into the streaming flow of water, joining my love, who is already as wet as a seal. We stand there together, while who-knows-what germs are washed away. I wonder what kinds of bacteria, now flowing toward the drain, made the trip from the hospital to our home on my husband's body, as we revel in each other's presence, in this fun, intimate way of saying "Hi, nice to see you."

I had no idea showers were so good for conversation. My love and I talk about education, broadly, and the idea of un-schooling, in particular. How would we have reacted to the freedom to learn at will when we were kids? What role does a positive culture play in the catalyzing forces of self-propelled discovery? What do each of our kids need to thrive, with their own particular personalities, predispositions, and unique expressions of life? If we homeschool, un-school, or otherwise educate without school, how could we integrate learning into the fabric of family life, as a natural expression of who we are and what's important to us? Where is the balance between the virtue of practice and the value of unhindered wonder? Or like I said in my last entry, the finesse of sensing when to interfere just a little, then zip it, and let life do what it does.

I have to say, it's our most energizing and fruitful conversation about the kids' education to date, and when we emerged dripping wet from the shower, I mentioned that our talk was sort of a quintessential expression of un-schooling, because it wasn't planned, there was no agenda, it happened spontaneously out of the attraction and engagement of two intelligent individuals who care about something in common and who happened to be in the shower, happily enjoying life together.

The conversation is so great, I'm late for class. Although being late makes me panicky, it turns out fine. After the teleclass, I find my love curled up on the bed in the cutest, snuggliest position. I wiggle in.

I won't tell you what happens a few minutes later.

47

It's Raining Men

April 14th, 2010

The last notable time I heard the song, "It's Raining Men," I was in Montreal, about five years ago, at a Karaoke place with my love. My little brother babysat Nika at our hotel, and Gabe and Avsi weren't here yet. A group of drunk guys was guzzling beer and grooving, and I could easily picture them falling from the sky. I wouldn't want to get squished by one of them, on the way down. The next song up was "You're My Angel," by Shaggy. My love sang it to me, and I danced for him on stage. Hardly anyone watched, because they were guzzling beer with their friends and didn't care, which was fine with us. We were just fresh in love and happy to be together and also happy that it didn't start raining men on our heads.

This week the song is playing notably inside my head, and I am seriously imagining fat ones, skinny ones, bald ones, men working at their desks, sitting on the toilet, men mid-sentence on the phone, men wearing striped pants, men with dumbbells from the gym, men wearing only socks, men holding plates of spaghetti, all falling innocuously from the sky. Lately it seems like it really is raining men and they are landing in my path, some more innocuously than others.

It's Tuesday morning and I'm at the coffee shop, sitting on a stool, into in a book by Hazrat Inayat Khan, called *Being and Becoming*. Kahn uprooted Sufism from its Islamic origins and re-planted it in a more universal Westernized context. Khan also founded a Sufi commune, called The Abode, where I was born at home, in an octagonal log cabin. I visited The Abode, now populated with a dwindling community of aging hippies, when I turned 16. I sat in a private retreat room and thought about life and its possible meaning, and how badly I wanted to meet my soul mate. I used pastels to draw a picture of me and my soul mate finding our way to one another, held in a ball of light. I wondered if I would ever meet him. I tried, unsuccessfully, to meditate, but thoroughly enjoyed the savory vegetarian entrées brought to my sparse and warm room at breakfast, lunch, and dinner. An adviser came to me once, at midday, to talk. I asked her: "What is God?" She said, "God is like a diamond with many facets." I was unsatisfied. It sounded so true and yet so unhelpfully vague for a teenager desperate for truth and certainty.

After my retreat, I visited the communal kitchen, where I once played under the table with my first friend, Katrina. I was 18 months; she was two. I worshiped the living daylights out of her. I got to meet an old friend of my mom's and then we headed home. A few months later, I became a fundamentalist Christian. A few weeks ago, I decided it was time to pick up Hazrat Inayat Khan's work, which I'm finally getting around to now that I'm sitting on my comfy stool at Lovejoy Bakers.

A familiar-looking man is seated on his own stool nearby, glancing casually at the local paper. After one has seen a face in a coffee shop for long enough, it seems civil to make small talk, so I ask the guy if he's reading anything interesting.

"Not really," he says. "What are you reading?" This leads to a fascinating and innocuous conversation, starting with the guy's friend who likes Sufi poetry, arcing into the territory of what we each do for work (he buys and sells companies), and coming full circle to a philosophical exchange about string theory. If a string vibrates (movement) and the vibration is sound, which comes first, music or dance? And if you can't actually separate sound and movement, could it be that the music and the dance are one? I think in this case, the chicken is the egg. Either way, it's an enlivening, yet innocuous discussion.

Welcome to Wednesday morning: I'm walking home after a fundraising meeting for a local non-profit. In front of Rite Aid, I spot a kid sitting on the sidewalk with a cardboard sign inked with "Anything helps." The boy, who looks about 14 to 18 years old, has his face lowered, eyes closed, in the posture of humiliation and withdrawal I've seen in the body language of countless homeless people around town. Except this looks like a kid who hasn't been this way forever. He looks ... newly hopeless. I have a feeling the lights are still on in there, that someone is home who just doesn't know how to get out.

"I'm not going to give you money," I say, "but here's my card. I'm a life coach and I'd love to do a free session with you. You can do more than this with your life."

His eyes perk up, as he takes my card.

"Can I call you?" he asks. I suggest to the young man that he call my business line at 8:45 p.m., to schedule a session. Silently I wonder what type of phone access he has. Then I realize I haven't gotten his name, so I ask:

"What's your name?"

"Phil," he says.

"Nice to meet you, Phil. I'm Alicia." I smile genuinely, but do not shake his hand, which is probably irrational since studies have shown fecal bacteria to be on the hands of average people who live in homes.

It's 7:35 on a Wednesday evening. I'm out for an hour of time to feel my own space, while one of our new sitters holds down the fort and folds the laundry. Strolling along on the sidewalk, soaking in the warmish-cool evening air, and doing some conscious breathing, I notice how when I lift up from my core, my shoulders drop and the whole world seems lighter from the inside out. I smile.

Out of the blue, someone says, "You must be having a good day—look at you smiling! I just had to stop you and know who is this girl who is smiling for no apparent reason?" I tell him I'm a life coach, and about my three kids and my adoring, wonderful husband and about how nice it is just to breathe in and out on a beautiful day. I find out he is a former homicide detective who worked for the state. He tells me a lot about his life and how he loves his wife, but they are separated and he's probably losing her. The guy wonders aloud, "I don't know why I'm telling you this." I tell him how maybe life coaching can help him. He asks if I coach at wine bars. We exchange cards. I wonder if he's innocuous, or not. I'm unsure.

It's late Wednesday night. My love is on-call. The kids are asleep, after a lovely day, full of hugs and horsey rides, and a family picnic, including Daddy, at the Tanner Springs. It's been a satisfying day and I'm tired. I look tired. I hoist the trash over my shoulder, exit our apartment, lock the door, lug the trash down the hall, and heave it down the garbage shoot into the abyss of who-knows-where.

On my way home, I run into a guy from our building I haven't seen for a while. I used to know his name, but it's inaccessible, because my brain is toast.

"ALICIA!" he says, like he is announcing my name at an event.

"You'll have to remind me—"

"Austin. Like Austin the Awesome. What are you doing to tonight?"

"I'm reading a book and going to bed," I say.

He harangues me. "BOOORING."

I say something about the value of books and how they can change the world and how they put me in my happy place. He goes along with it and says something about the power of positive thinking and premonitions.

"What are you up to?" I ask to be polite.

"I'm watching a movie over here in 229 with my friend Jon the Mon. You want to come?" I hesitate. Is it a good idea? I conclude that since I haven't had much of a purely social life in while, it might be good for me to get out and just to stop by. I'd only be a few doors down from my apartment and I'll only stay a few minutes. Put in an appearance, then go home and find my bed before the little ones find me missing from it.

I return home to pour myself a mug of hot chocolate, which has been heating up on the stove, and to spend a few minutes with my book, to unwind. I also ask for higher guidance. "Go with caution" is the word.

I head over to the home of Jon the Mon, who is a large chain-smoking man in his fifties, with a red beard and a lot of motorcycle paraphernalia. A decision is unanimously made to move the party over to Austin's house, which is a welcome relief, since Jon the Mon's place reeks of tobacco.

Austin's studio is a prototypical bachelor pad: reasonably neat and clean; slight smell of smoke, but not overpowering; a glowing neon sign that says "Mission Burrito" on the wall, which he got when his old employer decided to change the name of the business; and little tiki torches on the porch, also from the same former employer. Austin has, apparently, been going job to job and his plan is to "take a break" and go on a motorcycle trip across the West Coast, with Jon the Mon, of course, who it turns out, used to build bridges, including the one that goes to the zoo. Jon the Mon is retired. His closest relationship appears to be with his Harley. I ask the two of them, "Why the trip?"

Austin explains that Jon the Mon has a brother he wants to see in California. Then Awesome Austin points to a photo on the wall of him sitting opposite a gorgeous, sultry woman, who from a distance, looks like Marilyn Monroe wearing black leather short shorts. I discover through inquiry that Austin and this girl met on Myspace, but now they know each other in real time, too. The girl is a nurse, "but a sexy nurse," as Austin explains. The sexy nurse lives in California. She and Austin are friends, but he *could* fall in love with her. I can't tell if the sexy nurse is Austin's reason for the road trip, or his excuse for it. Or maybe it's like the chicken that is the egg, or the vibration that is both the sound and the movement. Perhaps Austin needs the excuse to be the reason. Oddly, every other sentence, Austin tells me how pretty I am, and then apologizes for it. The whole thing is odd, because, in addition to the fact that I look nothing like the sexy nurse, Austin sees me walking around with my three kids and my man. I get the concept that a woman

ALICIA KWON

with one kid looks like a good candidate for fertilization because she's proven her reproductive prowess—but three? With the family intact? Odd. Its gets stranger. Austin invites my whole crew—kids, husband, everybody—to his upcoming birthday party, which is to be hosted by his friend, who is "the" PDX Speed Dating coach, and lives in a posh loft behind the post office. I thank him for the invitation. As I walk toward the door, he tells me again how pretty I am, and I remind him that my husband might treat him in the hospital someday, so it would be good for him not to mess with me. "I'm gonna go now," I say, as I open the door.

"Jon the Mon, stop making her feel uncomfortable!" says Austin, in a flirty, teasing voice. "Jon the Mon isn't making me feel uncomfortable," I say as I walk out.

Once I'm safely back in my apartment, home before the little ones ever noticed I was absent, I settle in with my book again. I'm reading *10 Principles for Spiritual Parenting,* by Mimi Doe with Marsha Walch, Ph.D., who is Mimi's mom. What a welcome relief to savor words about wholeness and holiness and carpools, after such an unexpectedly weird experience.

Thursday night. I check messages and Phil, the homeless kid, has left one! A day late, but he called! I'm elated—really didn't expect him to follow through and call. I press "88" to call the sender and wonder what line I'll reach. Phil answers the phone, sounding as intelligent as any young person, albeit a young person with some problems with figure out. In a nutshell, Phil reports that he had a job and an apartment, but lost the job, then the apartment, then his two little kids, who are Phil's only family in the area. The children are, in fact, the reason why Phil is homeless in Portland, instead of having a place to land temporarily with his own parents elsewhere. Phil's father pays for the cell phone. These days Phil is living at a religiously based youth shelter. Don't ask how someone young enough to live at a youth shelter has a five-year-old and a two-year-old, but it is what it is. Phil tells me this is the first week that he didn't look for a job. What he really wants is to get an education, and to get his kids back.

I schedule Phil for a coaching session on Friday, the 23rd, at 9:30 at Starbucks in Pioneer Square.

48

A Rectangle with a Cat in It

April 20th, 2010

Small hands wrap around a plastic cup of orange juice and a little face appears unbelievably peaceful as it looks off into space, as though watching heaven float by on a fluffy white cloud. It is as if Gabe's whole body has lightened, and even though he isn't much for talking, the contentment is evident in his twinkling eyes and lax body. I'm sitting across from my little boy at Camellia Tea Zone. We are celebrating our new tradition of Monday afternoon dates.

Getting here has been quite the journey, literally, and metaphorically.

Intern year has been tough on Gabe. Lately, he wants Mommy and Daddy to stay with him "all the days and all the nights." It is as if he is on guard against the inevitable separations that are part of our life. An hour or two away from Mommy is devastating because it is in the context of days on end when he may or may not see his dad. Even as an adult, it's taken me three-fourths of the way through intern year to finally feel like I'm in an emotional equilibrium where I can flex and thrive happily. Over the weekend, our guy was home for two days in a row, which is like finding a quartz crystal in a driveway, not totally unheard of, but pretty rare.

On Saturday we hosted Avsi's friend's birthday, which was full of lovely people whom we all like very much. I'm pretty sure the adults had at least as much fun as the kids. Two of the grownups slid down the railing at Tanner Springs for the first time, for one thing, and everyone who came was just exactly the kind of people you hope to hang out with as a part of life—fun, wholesome, multicultural, intelligent, spiritual, open-hearted, zesty. We ended the party a little past noon, and our friend/sitter stayed and watched the kids for an hour and a half while my love and I enjoyed a fun rendezvous at Fat Straw, where we sucked tapioca through a straw and sipped a white mocha to the last drop.

We spent the late afternoon with new family friends who we met through the Internet. Or more accurately, I am on this parent coach's awesome online newsletter, called the Daily Groove, which gives pointers on parenting using the Laws of Attraction, and when I saw that he and his family just moved to Portland, I called the dude up and said, "Hey," which led to a family get together, consisting of us, him, and his wife and their two girls, one of whom is about Nika's age.

On Sunday we hung out, just our crew, doing things like playing a family game of Sorry! and watching the Mama and Daddy ducks at Tanner Springs. My love and I snuck out for another hour and a half to chill with each other. He read to me from *What the Dog Saw,* and we talked about ideas and life and our kids. And we laughed together. In the evening, we loaded up everybody to drive around Portland, exploring possible neighborhoods for the someday when we are ready to find a home that is, as Gabe put it, "somewhere between a cottage and a big house." In the evening, when we tucked everyone in, Gabe reiterated his theme song: "I want Daddy and Mommy to stay home all the days and all the nights and I don't want Daddy to go to work or be on-call any of the days." He punctuated his statement with a grunt at the end, for emphasis.

I may not be able to grant his wish of 24/7 Mommy and Daddy, but at least I can make a more regular habit of creating little sanctuaries of undivided attention to strengthen the security and interconnectedness that weave together the fabric of his internal tapestry. Gabe picked Monday as his date day, and so, from the first thing in the morning today, we have been preparing for the literal journey to our sanctuary of time together.

First there was waking Nika from a super-deep slumber in time to head for school to learn about forest ecology and outrun all the boys on the playground. Then there was the walk to drop off Avsi at WeVillage, our neighborhood's posh drop-in "urban playcare" center, owned by a fabulous single mom with a son in Nika's class.

A few blocks from home, it is abundantly apparent that the green hand-me-down boots that Avsi picked out to wear today are officially 112 sizes too big and completely doomed to fall predictably off Avriana's small feet every time. By the time we reached Johnson Street, I tucked Avsi's boots into my pocketbook, with the tops sticking out, and carried Avriana on my back, her little bare feet dangling just below my armpits.

Around Glisan Street, Avsi, Gabe, and I ran into Awesome Austin, the flirty neighbor who kept telling me how pretty I was, then apologizing for it the other night. Austin politely said "Hi" with the air of someone who is trying hard to act professional and respectful. At least he was trying— I'll give him credit for that.

When I told my love about the odd situation with Awesome Austin the other night, my husband was mildly annoyed that someone was hitting on me. However, noting that he wasn't threatened, I decided to get some playful extra mileage out the occasion. "Well, just so you know, it turns out I can say anything I want and get away with it 'cause I'm pretty. That's what Awesome Austin said, so it must be true." My love laughed with or probably at me on that one. Then I got tickled. Of course, my love doesn't relish the idea of other men digging his wife, but he's just not usually the jealous type. I, on the other hand, feel unnerved by the mere thought of my husband performing a pelvic exam on a woman with a possible STD or checking the cervix of a lady in labor. It just gives me the conceptual creeps. Like even if it's totally professional, what's my guy's hand doing in *her* zone? Interestingly, as a loyal, liberal person with a high degree of professionalism and respect for women, my love's innate sensibility is that, all things being equal, it would seem more fitting to have a female physician or midwife address the medical issues pertaining to a woman's intimate tissues.

Of course, by the time the kids and I got to WeVillage, I had to push out thoughts of my husband performing pelvic exams on other women, as well as head-shaking bemused wonderment about Awesome Austin, because I had to focus on signing-in, giving the caregiver instructions on allergy-free snacks, making sure to give Avsi the perfect amount of hugs and kisses (she's very particular about how many she wants), and digging out a pair of purple socks from my purse, recalling that foot-wise, it's not clothing optional at WeVillage.

At last, Gabe and I made it out, just the two of us, and walked two doors down, to Tea Zone, which is where I am savoring the peace in his angelic little face, watching him ease the orange juice up his straw in unselfconscious bliss. We enjoy sharing a gluten-free brownie, and I sip a skim chai. In the space of 5 minutes, I manage to knock over the sugar container twice, while Gabe, who is usually the clumsiest Kwon, doesn't knock over anything. He is quite serene, basking in this zone of unconditional presence and intentional togetherness.

I pull out a notebook from my purse and begin doodling some words and pictures for my son. He doesn't like the kitty I make for him, which is surprising. He wants me to draw him a rectangle. "Do you want me to put the kitty inside the rectangle?" I ask. Gabe's little face lights up. "Yeah!" He giggles exuberantly. "I want you to draw a rectangle and put the kitty in it!" I do my best. When my little drawing is complete, Gabey counts the sides of the rectangle: "One, two, three, FOUR!"

After a while, I invite my little guy to come sit on my lap. With earnest care, Gabe scoots his plate and orange juice to the spot in front of me, before making his own way around the table and into a lap-hug. Gabey and I sit happily doing nothing for a while. It is very peaceful. Until I remember it's Monday, which means that Nika has French, which means I'm supposed to pick her up, like almost now. For some reason, I had it in my head to get home in time for her to hop off the bus. Oops! I scoop up Gabe and practically leap over to the cash register to pay our bill.

I yank out my card, and adjust Gabe on my hip. The cashier looks puzzled as she looks at the register from behind the pastry counter. "Your card was declined," says the woman.

Oh man! It suddenly occurs to me that last week I lost my wallet for a few hours, then found it in the kids' room lying on the floor like a misappropriated toy. In the intervening time, I canceled all my credit cards.

And here I am, late and cashless. I scrounge around in my bag for *something*. Turns out I have one check left in my checkbook, which randomly happens to be in my bag, thank God. It's my lucky day, because although it's not their normal policy, Tea Zone takes my check and lets me go free. So we're off. Gabe snuggles into the crook of my neck as I carry him hurriedly and happily toward WeVillage. "I love you Mom," he croons. "I love you too, sweetheart. So much."

At WeVillage, I scoop up Avsi, and once again stash her over-sized boots in my bag for safekeeping. I'm 4 feet out the door when I realize I haven't paid yet. I'm 5 feet out the door when I realize it isn't going to happen today. I couldn't have paid if I tried: I'm card-less, cashless, and check-less. Interestingly, no one asked for payment when I thanked them very much and headed out. I figure it must be understood by a higher power that while I cannot pay today, I'll be good for it tomorrow. Luck seems to materialize when you let go of control and celebrate the offbeat ways that the Divine is cavorting to help us out.

In the evening, Nika and I snuggle up for our weekly episode of *Emily of New Moon.* Pillow propped up with red, blue, and black cushions from IKEA, Nika and I cuddle into each other contentedly, at ease and enjoying one another's company. This episode's story line is about a mentally ill man who was conceived "on the wrong side of the blanket," as they say on old-fashioned Prince Edward Island. The man is both feared and ostracized by the locals, and at the end of the episode, Emily writes in her journal, "I thought he was a serpent, but he turned out not to be a serpent, but a terribly lonely, sad man." That line sticks with me.

I scoop up my oldest little girl, who is almost as tall as I am, and carry her like a baby to her bed. I feel like the character in the story about the boy who started carrying a newborn calf and kept carrying it as it grew, so that eventually he was able to carry a full-grown cow. My lovely oldest daughter has no cow-like features. However, I do wonder if I'll keep getting buffer as she gets bigger, if ever a day will come when I find I have to hang and tell her to walk. In the meantime, I am so lucky.

With all the children asleep, there's a peace about the completed day, and the only thing that is missing is my love. He'll be back tomorrow, at about 2 o'clock.

49
Temporary Insanity

April 29th, 2010

The online Free Dictionary defines *insanity* as "a degree of mental malfunctioning sufficient to relieve the accused of legal responsibility for the act committed." I don't know if it's astrological—I have a friend who is into that who says that things are crazy for everyone she knows this week, and she is convinced it's because Mercury is in retrograde. Or it could be that with air pressure, or just the pressure inside my head, but this week things have just felt "off." In the space of two days, I have inadvertently knocked over, and shattered, an unopened olive oil jar, and splattered a brimming-full cup of smoothie all over the kitchen, including the walls, fridge, and the nasty little corner crevices behind the vitamin tray. I'm klutzy, but not usually *that* much of a moving accident waiting to happen. There have been other weird incidents too.

On Friday, Phil, the homeless kid I offered to coach for free, showed up, perfectly on time for his appointment. He even called 10 minutes ahead of the appointment to say he might be 5 minutes late, even though he made it for our scheduled meeting. Then the problems began. I guess he had been to the ER the previous evening and been prescribed valium for panic attacks. Phil's story goes that he took two before our session, as indicated on the label. The thing is, he started experiencing a rather intense and apparently

unexpected reaction, which included, but was not limited to, drool-
ing all over his cell phone, while trying to show me pictures of beautiful kids, attempting to scoot his chair closer to mine, while asking
if I had a boyfriend or a husband (I told him I have a wonderful
husband), and blathering on about how he is lonely and wants to
find someone pretty and sophisticated ... like me.

I have never seen anyone so crestfallen to find out that I'm happily married—the guy was really bummed. I tried to tell him that
getting his life together would be a good step toward a healthy relationship with a great girl ... other than me. Since proper coaching didn't seem feasible, I scribbled a few suggestions for him on a
piece of paper, set some hardcore boundaries around appropriate
behavior for any future coaching, and instead of hooking him up
with me, I made my best efforts to connect him with some great resources from a friend of mine who works with people coping with
drug addiction and mental health challenges while trying to transition out of homelessness. Then I excused myself, walked home,
and got in my car to pick up the little ones from preschool, slightly
shaken.

Saturday, so far, was turning out to be an exercise in living
through one of those horrible days that leave a well-rested person
tired and a tired person temporarily insane. Have you ever mustered
every creative fiber in your being and found that absolutely nothing you do has any effect on the people around you who are falling
apart or trying to kill one another in front of your very eyes? It's
one of those days. Oh it's that time of month, and of course my love
is on 30-hour call, and everything is going to hell in a hand-basket,
in spite of my best efforts at eliciting collaboration, de-escalating
conflicts, and surviving an onslaught of full-on tantrums from Avsi,
in which she is unflinchingly convinced that the only thing that will
make her feel better is to bite me, plus siren-like perpetual whining
from Gabe, Mommy-limit-testing by Nika, replete with smart-aleck

antics, topped off by a virtuoso performance turned in by all three, bringing to life Shakespeare's unknown not-funny comic tragedy, "The Kwon Siblings Fight to the Death." I can be a really good parent until my cortisol levels get to a certain point. Then I better put myself in time out, for the safety of everyone. By one o'clock in the afternoon, I'm freaking toast. Like the kind of toast that is completely burnt, more black than brown, with sooty edges. I'm unbearably crumbling, giving in to the sooty part of me that just hates, hates, hates the fact that so much of my existence is *this*.

I go in the bathroom to cry, and as if on cue, the towel rack clatters to the floor with a crash. I guess the fact that I slammed the door with the force of Hurricane Katrina probably contributed to that outcome.

I let out a loud noise that probably sounded like a cross between the moan of a woman giving birth and the wail of a wounded animal. I feel like both.

Eventually, when I've settled down, the little two plop in my lap and the oldest comes in to lecture me. We take turns at the lectern. It's my turn, and I'm on a strong rant about her problematic attitude, when my almost-eight-year-old smiles an offbeat smile and observes out loud: "Hey, my tooth just fell out!"

The two of us have a good ironic laugh. Nika's teeth fall out at the most unlikely times. One fell out during the ceremony of her Daddy's medical school graduation; another tooth fell out in a taxi van on the way home from the airport. Now this. If she could market "How to Make Your Tooth Fall Out in the Middle of a Parental Lecture," I think it would sell well among today's child population.

Twenty minutes later, I wipe my tears and wonder if I have swollen eyes as I open the door for the art therapist, who is coming to do "Creative Day" with the kids. We are exchanging coaching for Creative Day. I feel totally unprofessional today, and in fact I'm convinced this woman is going to find my three children traumatized and declare me an unfit mother, which is what I feel like, truth be told.

I head out for an hour to walk among the flowering trees and inhale softly, letting my breath out to find my center while I wait for the gluten-free pizza I have ordered for takeout. I am so tired and so thankful for a chance to decompress, I don't even care what the art therapist thinks. I'm just overjoyed to have a few moments of peace to help me go home with a little more sanity to share with my family. When I return home, the art therapist tells me that the kids are happy, internally organized, and smart. Her goal is to help them come together as a team. Her only concern was about Gabe, who wanted to trace letters and numbers instead of participating in the creative activity. I personally have no idea how the kids spring back from hell so well, but I'm glad the only problem a professional sees is that one of my kids likes math and English better than art. I'm happy for storms that have dispersed into clear skies. Everything passes.

In the long-awaited evening, when cleanup is complete, I read to Gabe and Avsi until their exhausted eyes close and their droopy heads conk out, one leaning up against my ribs, the other sprawled out on my leg. I sit for a few minutes, witnessing their little bellies freely rising and falling with the in-and-out rhythm of sleep. In time, I carry them into their own room and kiss them each on the forehead, feeling the contented return of sanity.

I come into the living room, where Nika and I pull out the couch into its bedlike shape and cozy up for an episode of *Emily of New Moon,* relaxing into each other's unfettered company, lectures far from our minds. When my big girl is asleep, and my own eyes are beginning feel irresistibly heavy, I remember the fact that I have Tooth Fairy duty. I put on my imaginary wings and leave under my oldest little girl's pillow a dog-themed charm bracelet and a white stretchy headband with sown-in clear rhinestones.

50
Munch, Wiggle, Poop, Love

April 30, 2010

In the morning on Sunday, when my love arrives home, haggard yet happy after his latest call shift, he offers me the opportunity to get outside on my own, stretch in the sunshine, and breathe in the effortless space of having to do nothing. I lay like a starfish on the soft green grass, still slightly damp, at Tanner Springs. As a wet spot seeps into my pants from the dew, I feel gratitude flushing out everything old. On my way home, I pick up a Tooth Fairy present from Green Frog, for Nika has yet *another* loose tooth dangling in her mouth.

After lunch as a family, my love lays down on the couch. I'm taking Avriana on a mother-daughter outing. First, we head to Goodwill, where I snag a pair of sweatpants that will work for NIA, which is a form of movement fitness inspired by dance, yoga, and tai chi. Avsi ever-so-gently holds my sweatpants as we make our way through the aisles of used clothing toward the register. Once the pants are paid for, the two of us go out for frozen yogurt. Avriana and I share a cup of Vanilla Cinnamon with juicy bright strawberries on top. We pretend our compostable cups are a pair of mother-daughter horses, making them talk to each other in funny voices. The cup-horses nuzzle and kiss. Avsi and I try to ignore the homeless guy outside the window who is slowly raising and lowering his middle finger at another homeless guy. Avsi clues me into the fact that her favorite current book is *The Fairy Tale One*. When we have scraped and licked our cups clean, we place them, along with our corn-based utensils, in the compost. The compost reminds Avsi of when we went as a family to help out on a local farm recently. She says, "Mommy, remember the song the girl at the farm made up about the worms?"

"Yes, that's a fun one!" I say.

"Munch, munch, munch. Wiggle, wiggle, wiggle. Poop, poop, poop," we chant together as we walk out the door.

On our way home, we pick up takeout from Laughing Planet to share with everyone at home. A fun beat is playing on the loudspeaker, and while we wait, my littlest girl and I dance to the music. Our movements feel light and silly. Life is effervescent. A curvy woman with streaks of gray in her hair is in line next to us, and as if our groove is contagious, she starts moving to the beat, adding another layer to our harmony. Suddenly shy, Avsi looks up at this stranger and dashes behind my leg, holding on to my shirt with her little fingers.

Once our order is placed, I scamper outside and descend into a thick grove of bushes with little stones for a floor bed. Avsi plops in my lap.

In a few minutes, our food is ready and we carry it two blocks home. The evening is lovely. Our table is filled with an enjoyable quiet as five happy campers chew yummy bites of beans, rice, and veggies, and savor family time. Somewhere about halfway through supper, Nika's other loose tooth falls out. Thankfully, I'm Tooth Fairy–ready.

When our plates are empty, we play a round of "Telephone," and have a great time, followed by a round of "The Minister's Cat," which engages our oldest, while the littler ones hop off to do their own thing.

Everyone helps out with cleanup unusually well. I teach Gabe how to wipe the crumbs from the table into his hand. Then, while my love helps Gabe and Avsi prepare for bed, I read to Nika from one of her favorite Felicity books. Eventually, a pajama-clad Avriana lumbers over to join us, draping her body over my shoulder, so that she is hanging upside down like a sloth, her head full of chocolaty hair nuzzled in my lap. I'm happy as a clam with my two wonderful daughters. These two girls are among my favorite people in the world. Besides the fact I love them, I actually like them a whole lot.

Was it less than 24 hours ago that I was tearfully chanting in my head, "If this is what motherhood is, I think I don't want it!"?

I think life works better when we hold lightly the temporary insanity that each of us experiences from time to time as part and parcel of the human condition, allowing it to pass through and safely returning us to our underlying essence and sanity.

Once everyone under the age of eight is sleeping, my love and I huddle up together for a foreign chick-flick called *David and Leila*. It's the love story of a Jewish American guy (David), who owns a bachelor-oriented cable show, and a young Muslim woman, a Kurdish refugee named Leila, whose family has been gassed by Saddam Hussein. Leila has 30 days to get married "for real" or else face deportation, and it just so happens that a spark of love ignites between the two, in spite of the protestations of their families. I love the film for its nuances, tasteful zest, and sensuality, its history, joy, and humor, and, of course, its happy ending.

My love and I enjoy a happy ending to our evening, too.

51

Paternity

May 3rd, 2010

A white woman gives birth on the L & D floor of the hospital where my husband is doing his OB rotation. My love helps this woman deliver a healthy, totally Caucasian-looking infant. Outside the room, an entourage of eager and supportive darker-skinned Latinos awaits the news of their newest family member's arrival with excitement and great anticipation. Grandmother is there, of course. She explains why her son, the father of the baby, had to miss the birth due to work obligations. It's his first job after nine months of unemployment. According to Grandma of the new arrival, her son is a little bit of a slacker.

There's information that Grandma doesn't know.

Well, first off, Grandma isn't technically Grandma, if we're talking about pure biology. Her son's sperm didn't impregnate the mother who popped out the baby, which explains why the infant looks totally Caucasian. It's not that the mother is easy or unfaithful either. Instead, the baby is a byproduct of rape, and Grandma's son has agreed to step up and parent this precious little person with such an unfortunate start in life.

Grandma's son is a hero. He knows the truth and is willing to be this child's father. The entourage in the waiting room, well they have no idea. They assume this baby is genetically linked to *la familia*.

The social worker on the case wonders how long this couple will be able to keep their secret with that baby looking as white as the snow on Mt. Hood. As for me, I wonder if Grandma would think of her son as a slacker if she knew he was intentionally embracing the responsibility of parenting a child conceived from a coercive sex act between his girlfriend and some slimy other guy.

How would Grandma feel, if she knew? Would she be proud and understanding? Would she see him as a potentially freaked-out, fundamentally good person, possibly even a minor saint? Or would she disapprove of his involvement in a situation he didn't catalyze with his own body? I wonder too why the girl and her boyfriend chose to hide their secret from *la familia*.

Perhaps, my love and I muse, by the time the larger family finds out, the baby will be integrated into the group, loved for who he is, rather than whose sperm he came from. Let's hope paternity is only the first word and not the last word, or the defining word, in this little person's life. I firmly feel that fatherhood cannot be reduced to a paternity test. I know it in my bones, because of what I've lived through as the mom of a kid who has two dads, and uniquely wonderful relationships with each of them. The other day, Nika said, "I love all of my parents exactly as much, just in very different ways."

When I think of the word *daddy,* I think of the man you would want to walk you down the aisle at your wedding, regardless of whether or not he was the one who shared fluids with your mother on the night you were conceived. Of course, Nika will have to pick for herself how she wants to walk down the aisle, if in fact she follows that path. I, for one, would smile if she someday walks with a father on each arm.

Here's to the dads who stay involved with their kiddos even when they stop being involved with their child's mother, and here's to the dads who would fail a paternity test, yet pass with flying colors the tests of parenthood, every day.

52

A Nobel Prize Winner and Uncertainty with a Cup of Tea

May 25th, 2010

I wake up Saturday morning, stunned, dazed, and stressed. I finally got around to watching the 2010 finale of *Grey's Anatomy*. If you haven't seen it, skip it, unless you are thick-skinned. If you are thin-skinned like me, you may find it more rewarding and less traumatizing to spend the 2 hours writing a letter to your congressman insisting on more effective gun control.

I'm feeling uncertain about the world today—every day, lately. On the streetcar, an older gentleman who manages a seafood restaurant noted that in his lifetime never has he seen so many catastrophes in such a short span: shootings, real and fictional, natural disasters, international strife, and on and on. I'm an optimist, by nature, but this is a little scary. Like, I never imagined wondering if my kids would get to grow up. I went to check my email this morning, and Yahoo news (which usually reports stuff like which celebrity wore the most unflattering outfit) just informed me that a plane went down in India, killing a lot of people. Of course, then there's the fact that the Euro just collapsed. Closer to home, what about the homeless guys I see on the corners and on the steps of forsaken businesses around town? Even though I'm looking out the window of my two-bedroom apartment on the posh scenery of the Pearl District, I wonder how long it can last—how long can islands of ease, relative safety, and loveliness built on questionable financial premises continue untouched by the throes of terror that rock innocent lives in our interconnected world? It seems like I'm submerged in a marinade of fear, with a sense of utter helplessness frying my nerves. I wish I could wrap my arms around the world and save it. I wish I could tell my kids that everything will be fine for them, with the confidence I'd be telling the unqualified truth. Certainty is a crock, I get it. I try to meditate on the truth that perfect love casts out fear, but I can't fully get the images of terror from my mind. Has that ever happened to you?

Our whole family is heading to the home of our friend Liz, one of our most cherished former babysitters, turned friend. We are getting together for a potluck. Liz lives in Southeast Portland in a house with a huge backyard garden. Squash, tomatoes, lettuce, chives, basil, and strawberries grow alongside yellow, blue, and pink flowers. If a catastrophe ever struck locally, Liz and her roommates would be likely candidates to save us, thanks to the abundance they grow in their enormous plot of earth. Irises and pink daisies seem placid and strong, as if announcing that in spite of the news, life is flourishing. Liz guides us to the strawberry patch, which is just beginning to bear fruit, and each of us picks a singular strawberry. Then our entire crew tromps inside to munch on homemade hummus, quinoa salad, cranberry-nut-salad, gluten-free pizza, and gluten-free chocolate-chip cookies, which, by the way, are incredible. I ask Liz where she got the recipe and she shrugs with a smile. "Online."

Liz's house is filled with pets, including three cats, named Sercy, Hades, and Kitty-Pie, and a service dog, belonging to one of her roommates. A sweet black lab, slightly hyper, incredibly loyal to her companion, Jess, who is visually impaired. I can't remember the dog's name for the life of me. While Avsi and Nika seem most attracted to the dog, Gabe coos endlessly at the kitties. "That kitty loves me!" intones Gabe with delight.

Periodically, I check the time instinctively. I'm trying to be fully in here and now, but I also want to make sure I get to my next appointment on time, because it's a once-in-a-lifetime opportunity. I'm going to see Nobel Peace Prize winner Muhammad Yunus, the father of microcredit and the social business model. My love is dropping me off at the Baghdad Theatre, while the kids hang out with Liz for a little while. We have to leave at 1:30.

When the time comes for my love and I to depart, Gabe decides to take the trip to Baghdad with us, while the girls chill with Liz. When we arrive at the theatre, my love pulls up curbside and drops me off. I wave to my boys, as I step out into the pouring rain and scamper toward an old movie theater, indicating the shows and times in red lettering. Right below MUHAMMAD YUNUS - 2 P.M. is ALICE IN WONDERLAND - 5 P.M.

Once inside the theater, I see a variety of young professionals and middle-age intellectuals milling around the lobby. Lots of distinguished graying curls, bald heads, and semi-eccentric scarves. Many guests are already seated inside the theater to hear one of the truly great individuals of our time talk about a new form of capitalism, driven by the human instinct of compassion instead of propelled primarily by greed.

Yunus, who is Bangladeshi, comes on stage with a huge genuine smile and immediately cracks a joke the cultural accommodations made on his behalf: "The event coordinators even planned a monsoon to help me feel more at home!" Listening to Yunus speak about how his model of social business is lifting people out of poverty all over the world makes my skin tingle. This ordinary, sensible, huge-hearted guy started out giving out $27 loans to 42 women and has since developed his model of social business to the point where there is some form of it found in every country on earth. Muhammad Yunus has a new business model that is brilliant

227

in its powerful simplicity and its infinite possibilities. The idea is that some Joe or Jane or Ahmed or Irina observes a human need or a social problem. Then, instead of whining about it, this ordinary person uses their creativity, compassion, and joy to design a business that addresses the human concern in such a way that the business is self-sustaining, yet without consideration of profit margins. In this business practice, all profit, if there is any, either goes into expanding the business or into the pockets of the business owners if the owners are poor people who are being lifted up to a higher quality of life.

Success is measured exclusively in terms of how effectively the business addresses the concerns of the people or problem it was designed to benefit. Investors know upfront that if they loan a dollar, they get a dollar returned, in due time. Nothing more, nothing less. In this way, companies that use the social business model don't have to answer to boards that demand high profit margins. It's been found that 98 percent of the borrowers return the money. At Grameen Bank, the social business lender started by Yunus, 97 percent of the borrowers are women. That's because Yunus found that women are more likely than men to use the funds from their business to improve the life of the entire family. It's sort of ironic to see a wonderful man up there talking about how women do a better job at this sort of thing than men. It actually reminds me of my love who is convinced the world would be a better place if it were run by women. While I think a higher proportion of women in leadership positions would be an improvement over the current scenario in corporate and political America, I do think men do bring an important energy to the table, as long as it doesn't dominate.

Human nature is a funny topic to understand. Students have to write papers about it for intro to philosophy classes. The ones who get hooked on the question spend a lifetime parsing foreign languages and footnoting philosophical tombs with tiny print, and the rest of us live with the gnawing paradox of it all, right in our stomachs, every day. Whether we think about it consciously, or not, I think most people ache to understand their own inner selves, as well as the other people who make up the odd, wondrous, cruel, mundane, beautiful parade of humanity.

Which is our truest nature: good or evil? Or is our ultimate nature the position of choice between the two forces? Yunus critiques contemporary capitalism for its failure to recognize the fullness of our human character. While the usual form of capitalism literally capitalizes on greed and self-interest, Yunis insists with immense passion that human beings are multifaceted. We are both selfish and selfless. No one is just one or the other, yet our current system is based only on our selfish instincts. In Yunis's vision, the urge to take care of oneself and one's own is honored, while offering opportunity for the expression of our sense of empathy, interconnection, and our urge to help those less fortunate than ourselves.

Have you ever seen a huge bank owned by illiterate women that effectively loans out and recoups money to other poor women with an entrepreneurial spirit? Yunus made that vision a reality with Grameen Bank, and it's incredible to hear him talk about how these illiterate women who own the bank are seeing their children go on to higher education. When the young people get out of school, sometimes they come to Yunus and say, "We don't know what to do. Where are the jobs?" Yunus says, "Go talk to your mother. Your mother owns a bank. She can help you finance whatever you dream of creating. Don't be a job seeker; be a job giver. Don't be an employee; be an employer."

Listening to this guy is the perfect antidote for hopelessness and paralysis. You can't help but feel optimistic that it's feasible to impact formerly intractable problems. It just takes innovation in the hands of the right messenger at the right time, and a few willing people give the impossible a chance to morph into the actual through inspiration, creative problem solving, collaboration, and commitment.

Another thing I learn: All over the world, the banks founded on social business principles have been doing just fine throughout this financial crisis, whereas the profit-hungry, collateral-dependent giants next door fall and flail. Why is that?

Later, once the Yunus presentation is over and everyone has filed out of the theater, I stroll two blocks down in a wet drizzle to one of my favorite stops in Southeast Portland: Cup & Saucer. Here my love and I are meeting up eventually, once the kids are settled in with a wonderful sitter with whom I barter kid-care for coaching. A total win-win situation, I muse to myself, as I peruse the tea list. I settle on a cup of organic Lavender Lemon tea, which I order from my robust-looking waitress decked out in a turquoise skirt and wide-rimmed black glasses. While I start flipping through some of the pamphlets I pocketed on the way out of the theatre, and eventually dive into Yunus's latest book, various servers continue to refill my stainless-steel teapot with hot water. I'm unbelievably happy about unlimited tea!

I'm only a few pages into Yunus's new book, *Social Business,* when a familiar face peers at me through the window located behind me. I catch a glimpse from my peripheral vision and swivel around in my seat. Squishing his nose up to the glass is my love, and my heart feels light, like it may leap from my chest. For an unknown reason, I'm happily excited to see him in that flirty, in-love sort of way. I rise from my seat and meet him halfway between the entrance to Cup & Saucer and the booth where I've been immersing myself in ideas and tea. My love and I hug and kiss several times—gentle, firm kisses that border on making out—and then we are seated together.

It takes my love and I a while to order, because we have so much to talk over with each other. For starters, I'm thrilled to share my experiences and reflections on hearing Muhammad Yunus; then, of course, there's the unfortunate double traffic ticket that my love incurred on the way home from Liz's house. One for turning too late on a yellow arrow, the other for improperly installing Avsi's booster seat. Who knew? The funny thing is that in order to avoid having to pay the car seat ticket, my love has to sit through a 2-hour educational shtick at the hospital where he did his peds rotation, called "Trauma Nurses Talk Tough." Of course, learning to properly install your kid's seat is important, and I had no idea ours was improperly installed, but who can help but laugh at a re-education seminar called "Trauma Nurses Talk Tough"? I'm picturing a bouncer dressed in a nurse's uniform, or maybe skinny old-school nurses donning boxing gloves, revving it up on their Harley Davidson. Either way, my love and I laugh, though someone else will have to decide if it's because of the situation's innate humor, or more owing to our sense that laughter is exactly what the doctor ordered for us. Heaven knows, it's good to laugh freely with my love, and who the hell needs a reason for it? When two people are ready to laugh, the trigger is probably just an excuse to let the endorphins flow and the belly jiggle.

When the robust waitress with the turquoise getup and the black wide-rimmed glasses comes back, we finally order an avocado veggie burger sandwich, without the bun, and a fresh jasmine tea, unlimited refills promised.

53
Elementary Functions

May 27th, 2010

It's a Thursday afternoon, toward the end of an unusually rainy May. Last year at this time of year when our family stepped fresh off a plane that flew us from East Coast to West, we were met with lovely blue skies dotted with puffy white clouds. The spring of 2010 has been a little different. Now don't get me wrong, our February was eerily fantastic, weather-wise. It was warm and the sun shone and flowers bravely sprouted into premature bloom. March through May, on the other hand, has been an exercise in dreary patience and capricious winds. We have had an onslaught of cold rains, punctuated by arbitrary patches of open, sunlit sky, and here and there, literally out of the blue, we've felt hail pelt our heads.

Today is the first pretty day in a long time, and I get to do something uncannily normal: attend an elementary school function for our oldest kid, *with* my husband. Our daughter and her class are celebrating their end-of-the-year party a little early, because the teacher is going to be out for the rest of the year recovering from foot surgery. The kids will have a sub for the last two weeks of the academic year. Nika likes her own teacher a whole lot, but she has one good thing to say about the sub, who she has had before: The sub gives longer recesses.

It's the first time in a long time that my love and I have had the luck to attend one of Nika's events as a couple. Most of the video-camera moments coincide with when Daddy is on-call, which totally sucks. The one other time my love came to one of her school things since internship started, he swore up and down the wazoo that he'd be home by 6:30 to pick us up in time to drive over as a family to the second-grade's presentation of *The Selfish Giant*. My love (though I called him less adoring names that evening) was nowhere in sight, with no phone call when 6:30 came and went, so I had to pack the kids up by myself to get Nika there in the nick of time to put on her costume and join the rest of her class. I kept looking around the school, expecting to see him any minute, and after 45 minutes, I stopped looking and shut him out of my heart, temporarily. When that hubby of mine showed his face almost an hour late, it would have been better for both of us if he'd just stayed home. I was so mad I made him sit separately from me when he finally arrived. On top of everything, it was that time of the month. I did not handle things in a mature way.

What I learned, though, is that getting someone to swear up and down the wazoo is a recipe for betrayal, because you are putting your soul entirely outside yourself. Even God hasn't got complete control of everything, and the theory goes that God is wise enough to *choose* to be out of control for the sake of something more important, like love or free will. So what the hell have I been thinking all my life, trying to get people to swear to keep their promises to me, when it isn't ever in their ultimate control to do so? What do we get when we make people swear by promises? First, we get to feel entitled and in charge of life's rules. Then when someone who promised breaks our rules, we get to hate them, whether or not it was even their fault. Why do we treat hate like it's a privilege earned by our suffering when it just destroys us from the inside out? Acting like a punitive deity isn't healthy. Unfortunately, I seem to have to repeat this lesson often. I will probably have to take CE credits for my whole life on this one.

Even if I haven't got my own wisdom fully integrated, today I'm in luck, 'cause this elementary school function turns out fine and lovely, as my guy and I stroll across the grassy hill from car to classroom, arms linked, and in tune with each other. We enter portable Classroom 25 and look around wide-eyed, taking in the colors of second-grade wall decor, the smell of pizza and popcorn, and the sounds of semi-hyper kids on the loose. It's cool to see Nika in her "other" environs. We are amused and proud as we watch our oldest girl cruising around the room arm-in-arm with her best friend, Maki. We stand next to her worktable, observing, like completely biased scientists, how she balances eating popcorn and pizza with interacting socially. My love and I watch her inimitable reaction when a boy offers her his crackers. It's something in between polite disdain and innocent bemusement.

As the party winds down, my love and I thank our daughter's wonderful teacher, Miss Rosa. In the course of saying goodbye to a fellow parent, I mention all the fantastic qualities of Miss Rosa, and how wonderful and perfect she has been as a second-grade teacher for our kids. As an amusing afterthought, I casually mention how Nika said that while she'll be sad not to get to complete the year with Miss Rosa, she is excited because the sub gives longer recess. As fate would have it, at that very moment, who walks by? Of course, Miss Rosa. And I'm fairly certain she heard only the last part of what I said. I shove food awkwardly in my mouth, since it is difficult to reach my foot. After hugging Nika, my love and I drive off together to pick our little ones up from preschool. In a few short hours, my love will be back at work for the night. *Carpe diem.*

54

Professing Love to the Wrong Woman

June 4th, 2010

It's a Thursday afternoon and an exhausted, happy feeling washes over me. In spite of a long few months, I'm bathing in the thought that this will be my husband's last evening of night float for intern year, which is like the cornerstone of the beginning of the end of the this insanity. Once night float is over, my love has one last rotation to go, and it's just a month of ER, which everyone says is a fairly lightweight rotation in the scheme of things. I can feel the edges on my nerves smooth as I finally offer myself hard-earned permission to feel relief and optimism and to consider, as something that might apply to my family, the imminent possibility of a less demanding lifestyle. I snuggle into my napping love and nuzzle our cuddly little Gabe, who has joined us in bed for a snug.

Suddenly I smell something and it is undeniably odiferous. At first, I wonder if my sleeping Prince Charming has had too many beans for lunch. Within seconds, a girl appears in the doorway, clad in pink chiffon skirt, with matching pink velvet leotard. Her head is held high, her expression poised and totally matter-of-fact. She is the perfect picture of a little princess, except for the bulging weight sagging in her crotch.

I wait for her to speak first, which she does, with gusto.

"I pooped."

Now there is a clear pronouncement if there ever was one, from a princess or anyone else.

"Where?" I inquire, dreading the truthful response I'm sure to get from Avriana. I should be thankful for the innocence of transparency, but at this moment, honesty makes me cringe.

"I pooped some of it on the stroller and some of it in the living room and part of it is in the bathroom and there's also some in my undies."

Oy vey.

I follow the trail of brown smelly gooey lumps through an obstacle course covering the entire house circling finally back to its source. Lovely. I decide to start with the culprit, and clean up her trail later.

Avsi's wipe-down is an undertaking to say the least. On the plus side, my little poopy daughter stands there quite patiently, presenting her feces-covered areas for wiping and scrubbing. Eventually, Avriana is more or less de-pooped enough for a bath, and in she goes. I watch her pour water and soap on her terrycloth frog, cleaning him as I have just cleaned her. I wonder how much poop residue a microscope would find in the water that is "cleaning" her frog.

Cleaning the house is especially gross because I'm certain there is so much poop I'm sure to miss some little bit here or there, but I give it my best shot.

With that local mini natural disaster more or less put in order, I set about preparing for an evening out on the town. The plan is to meet up with our mutual friend Jane at Living Room Theater. My love is to join for a little while before he has to drive over to the hospital to get sign-out from the day team and start his last night shift. I'm doing some very minor primping in front of the bathroom mirror when my love walks in with a deep frown and forlorn downcast eyes that would leave a toddler's wide-eyed sad face in the dust any day.

"What's wrong?" I ask, feeling sympathetic and concerned over whatever is causing such forlornness to enter into my love.

"You know how there was that weird thing that was supposed to be at the end of the year that I told you about, well somehow it got switched around and I have to work tomorrow. I tried to get out of it and trade with someone, but I couldn't."

I feel the burn of tears. A feeling like being punched in the heart with disappointment. A feeling like it is personal, like the program must have somehow known that I had just mustered up the faith to feel it's okay to feel like the worst is over and they wanted to sock it to me one more time. It's irrational. I don't care. It feels true in this moment when my insides turn flips.

What makes this moment different from others like it is that in this moment my love and I reach for each other instead of for our boxing gloves. Instead of my enemy, this here person in the bathroom is my friend. The person I love. The one with whom I'm linked in body, heart, and essence. In this moment, I am in touch with the fact that I am happy about the link, even in times that seem stupidly unfair. My love and I hold each other, and it's okay that I'm crying, and he looks like his eyes are breaths away from letting out their salty waters too. It's okay to feel, okay to feel fully, in each other's presence, and to have feelings about that which formerly stood as the great impassable wall between us. Other presences join us in the bathroom.

Upon seeing me cry, Avriana looks at me intently, stretches up her arms toward me, indicating for me to pick her up, and wraps her entire being around me. "I love you," Avriana whispers. My little girl, my husband, and I hug each other for a while. Next, I take a firm deep breath, fix my eyeliner, wipe my teary cheeks, and give a few quick instructions to the sitter, who is waiting patiently in the living room, ignoring the drama in the bathroom.

On the way to Living Room Theater, I tell my love to phone our friend Jane to give her a heads-up that he'll be hanging out for a little while too, because Jane is under the impression that it's just going to be me. My love proceeds to dial Jane's number on his cell (since I don't have one) and leaves a voicemail, which sounds pretty ho hum, until he pauses at the end of it and says, "I love you, bye," and then looks at the phone like "What the ...?"

"Did I just say 'I love you'?" he asks, clearly disoriented, still looking at his phone in confusion.

"Yep, you did."

"That was really surreal. My brain is doing funny things. Well, don't worry, I don't feel any Eros love for her." *Eros* is Greek for "romantic or sexual love."

I'm laughing and crying at the same time, because I totally get it—when you or I or anyone is zombie-tired, you do things on autopilot, even when they don't make sense, or are situationally inappropriate. Who does he usually call and leave messages for? Me. What does he typically say at the end of a typical voicemail? "I love you, bye." So his sleep-deprived neurons have created an oversimplified equation: When leaving a message, end with saying "I love you, bye."

Whatever. This is what it has come to: My husband is so damn tired that he is walking around like a robot-zombie telling our friend "I love you, bye."

Jane calls back and says she is stuck at a meeting and will be late. She doesn't say anything about the weird voicemail. The upside of Jane's work situation is that my love and I get to sneak in a little date. Parking is scarce, so my guy drops me off curbside outside Living Room Theater so I can go ahead and enjoy the ambiance and order. We hardly ever have to deal with parking, living downtown, because usually we walk or take the streetcar, but since my love has to leave straight from our outing to go watch over patients hooked up to various machines, he had to bring the Corolla.

I seat myself at a cute little table with a couch on one side and chairs on the other. When our server approaches, I beg off the mandatory alcoholic beverage that is usually part and parcel of ordering off the happy-hour menu and order an acai white tea instead. I'm on a cleanse designed to help my overextended adrenals recover from the last few decades of life.

Within minutes, our sweetly skinny, eccentric, and almost certainly gay waiter sets down a lovely goblet of steaming white tea in front of me, along with a generous hummus platter, augmented with thick warm pitas formed into rounds. I sip the soothing liquid and scoop hummus onto a piece of pita I've gently torn and fold the savory mushiness into my mouth. Eventually, a handsome guy in scrubs walks in, smiles, eyes crinkling lovingly at me. The guy sits down at my table and I gaze at him lovingly back.

It's a treat to be together in the presence of yummy food and the conversation is interesting. I learn, for example, that the first official artificial life has been created. It's a DNA strand identical to that of a known bacteria that comes from a family of bacteria that can be harmful to humans. What were they thinking? So I guess now there's this constructed life form that if it mutated a wee bit could make people sick or kill them and it can independently replicate itself. I think to myself, Wow, another potential way for humans to destroy themselves, as I dip my pita bread into more hummus and look up into my love's eyes.

Sitting across from each other, holding hands and gazing, we abide in the depth of one another's deep lake soul windows for a long while. Perhaps imagining the possible end of the world as we know it is helping me keep at bay my own destructive emotions, at least temporarily.

Eventually our friend Jane shows up. I ask her if she heard my husband confess love to her. Jane says she thought that's what he said, but wasn't totally sure she heard the message right. I assure her that she heard correctly, and that my love is legally insane due to going more than 72 hours with less than 5 minutes of sleep at a stretch. My love nods and concurs, saying, "Yeah, um, sorry about that—I have never had anything like that happen. I'm most certainly out of my mind from being tired beyond anything I've experienced before." We all sigh and laugh. Then my love has to go. We kiss sort of wistfully, and in a whoosh of scrubs, he is off. I watch the silvery door of his car swing shut and try to ignore a pang I don't like one bit. It still feels like our weekend has been ruined, but at least in this moment there is the sweet presence of love as I watch him drive away into another world.

I linger and chat with Jane for a while. It's fun to catch up and talk over our thoughts on life, like how there aren't enough words or concepts for the different kinds of love there are on earth, and what makes a team magical, whether it's a corporate team or an intimate partnership, and how we are navigating the tricky waters of some challenges with our kids. Time flies, and before I know it, the clock strikes 9 p.m. Past my sitter's curfew! I'm a few minutes late home to a house full of kids who have been tucked in to sleep. I tiptoe, inhaling the quietude. Within minutes, one sleepy little boy pads down the hall and hops into the pullout bed in the living room and squirms until he has found the perfect position.

55

Kombucha and Rubber Chicken

June 25th, 2010

Tonight is the resident graduation for the third-year seniors, the ones who have made it out the other side of medical training and are being released into freedom, or at least greater freedom. I expect the lodge where the event is being held to be filled with dull speeches that aim at inspirational and land somewhere in the fancy pasta salad, along with elongated introductions and a long list of thank-yous to various people with whom I am unfamiliar. Graduation will probably feel meaningful in two years, when that's my love up there, but for now, it's blah, blah, blah, and I can't believe it's costing me an evening of extra childcare expense to shuffle my feet under a lacy table with a centerpiece. My love isn't enthusiastic either. We both figure it will be nice to show our faces and cheer for the folks who are done with residency; however, we are hoping to bypass some of the boring stuff by arriving considerably late.

Nora, our fantastic new nanny, shows up with a smile on her face and wishes us a great time. Her positivity is sort of contagious, and after plenty of hugs and kisses and last-minute things with the kids, my love and I are off, and we have a plan: to get snacks for just the two of us and show up late, hoping to bypass the most unbearably boring parts. Since the site of the graduation has the word "Lodge" in its name, I'm picturing a lot of non-organic meat and things fried in large vats. I'm hungry, so I figure some hummus and a Kombucha sound a lot easier on my body than what's likely to be for dinner. So my love and I talk it over and decide to hit up the natural foods store kitty corner from our apartment.

To get to Lil' Green Grocer from our home, all you have to do is meander through Tanner Springs urban park, and you're there. Inside, there are IKEA tables topped with baskets of individual pieces of organic produce, little aisles with everything from lavender soap to Bob's Red Mill flours. There is a whole wall of wine, a complete section devoted to chips, and several coolers: a small one for ice cream and ice-cream substitutes, and several longer ones for everything else that needs to be refrigerated: dairy, meat, deli takeout containers, and cool beverages. I'm scanning the beverage section searching for Kombucha. I look three times in its usual spot, just below the iced teas, to the left of the locally produced fruit smoothies. It's not there, like at all. Not even one bottle of the flavor that's not my favorite. Odd.

I first met and fell in love with Kombucha a few months ago, mesmerized by the fizzy, punchy, distinctive mingling of fruity and medicinal flavors in a fermented base reminiscent of a an ultra-light beer made for flower fairies. I was also enchanted with Kombucha's reputed health benefits ranging from sugar regulation to anti-aging properties. In addition to whatever objective healing properties you actually imbibe, you can't go wrong with a fabulous placebo effect to enhance the enjoyment of a cool beverage. So where has my Kombucha gone?

I march up to the front counter and in a friendly tone (after all, I like the owner of Lil' Green) ask, "What's the deal with Kombucha?"

The answer I get is that apparently, there's some question about the alcoholic content of Kombucha. The alcohol level is supposed to be less than 0.5 percent, but rumor has it that Lyndsay Lohan's Kombucha set off her alcohol monitor, tipping off a frenzy of investigations. The outcome, so the story goes, is that Kombucha is off the shelf for who knows how long until they can figure out how to control the alcohol content or re-label the stuff. Wow. What a great use of federal resources. Go after the Kombucha consumers. Oh my freaking goodness. The other night I witnessed a drug deal right outside my window, and when I called the non-emergency police number, the lady spent 5 minutes trying to figure out which side of the cross street the dudes were on, and before I finished telling her, they had driven off. The dispatch lady didn't want their license-plate number or care to know which way they went. But my gosh, if I'd said they were making Kombucha outside my window, I bet police would have headed straight over, to end the outrage of people who drink Kombucha, presenting such a danger to society that they may end up loitering around doing random acts of kindness and talking about the latest Green initiatives. That would be a threat to society as we know it.

Oh well. I share a good rant with the owner of Green Grocer, who is totally on our side. In addition to being a sane and nice person, his best-selling product is Kombucha. Sometimes life is just upside down.

In lieu of Kombucha, my love and I get some hummus, a package of Mary's Gone Crackers, and an organic 73 percent cacao chocolate bar. We cavort to take our snacks outside and nibble in the park. I lounge on my love while we snack, sunbathing in the last rays of the day.

In the weeks and days leading up to this one, I've asked my hubby about a thousand times if there will be dancing, or only food. I keep getting the same non-answer: "Well, I'm pretty sure there will be food ... and I think there may be music ..." The thing is, for me food and music is almost irrelevant without the opportunity to dance. Music without dance is like a writer being given a pen, or a laptop, without the opportunity to write.

In my soul, this is the ultimate: Freely grooving to the music, letting sound and energy swoop through my entire being, enrapturing me, or if I am with my love, us in its urge to express the inexpressible, in a meeting of the instinctual and the infinite, outside of time, in the immediacy of the moment. So you get that dance is sort of important to me—I can take or leave the live piano, or the classy jazz guy.

Gazing up at my hubby from a comfy position with my head in his lap, I ask him to promise me something:

"Promise me you'll dance with me even if there is no dancing?"

I can feel him fidget.

"Well Alicia ... I don't know. Let's see how it goes."

I give the face. You know *the face.*

He looks at me for a few moments. Then: "Okay, love, you win. I promise."

The smile spreading on my face is unstoppable.

"Thank you, love," I say, happy, giddy, truly filled with gratitude.

Eventually we leisurely make our way to the car, get in it, and drive, very slowly through traffic toward the resident graduation. We snack all the way through rush hour until we arrive at the lodge. I am pretty on target about the food: lots of greasy vegetables, potatoes, the ubiquitous rubber chicken, and some salmon that I'm pretty sure is not the Wild Alaskan kind that is non-toxic enough to eat. On the upside, the salad is unexpectedly delicious: lettuce dappled with cranberries, walnuts, and enough dressing to clothe a small nation in oil. I also decide to dig into the apple crisp because it looks like the speeches are in full force and I'm not sure I can endure this sort of thing without sugar.

Introductions, speeches, and presentations of various awards take up the rest of the evening, but it's not as bad as I feared. Of course, it's impossible for me make it the conclusion of an evening out without doing something mildly humiliating, and on this night, that moment comes when the program director says in an artificially hyped-up voice: "Let's all give a round of applause for our support staff, because YOU MAKE A DIFFERENCE!" I see some people stand up, and I figure it's a standing ovation. I'm all in favor of a standing O for a demographic that does a lot of scut work without the white-coat glory or the doctor's paycheck, so I stand and clap loudly.

My love looks at me, amused and says, "I didn't know you got a side job as a part of the support staff." I look around, and 85 percent of the others standing are nice, attractive young women in fitted floral dresses, with prom-like hairdos. The other 15 percent are pleasantly graying and a little plump, in a kindhearted-looking way. The whole group of them, young and older, is at one table, smiling like one unit, exchanging high fives here and there, along with glances of affirmation. I sit down and try to swallow the awkward feeling and minimize the redness creeping over me. I am a wife of an intern and I just stood up with the support-staff team. I am an idiot. Oh well. And so I resume listening to the unending procession of speakers. The unendingness of it is softened by the fact that several of the presenters are funny, and because some are funny in a sort of intimately cruel way, I have to assume that there is a deep connection among the physicians and the residents. Here is an

246

excerpt of an awards presentation for Faculty Member of the Year, made by a graduating resident:

"So when Dr. Flynn showed up for her interview three years ago, the first thing I saw was a woman in a denim skirt, like the kind I associate with people involved with fringe religions. And she was sitting on a desk. She looked really tired, like she had cancer or something (which she actually did at the time), and I wondered about her, and what the program had in mind when they hired her. But ever since Dr. Flynn came on board, things have just really looked up around here. So since you seem like kind of a woodsy girl, Dr. Flynn, we got you some camping accessories. Here (he hands her a bag of stuff that looks more like beach toys than camping equipment). Thank you Dr. Flynn."

Everyone claps appreciatively, including Dr. Flynn, who is smiling.

When the official event is over, the jazz band plays some songs while people circulate informally, saying "Hello" and "Nice to meet you."A young woman in a flowery dress comes over and touches my arm almost as if I'm special fabric and says, "You must be Dr. Kwon's wife. I'm Cathy, one of the medical assistants. I work at his station. We love Dr. Kwon. He's our favorite to work with, 'cause he's just so nice and wonderful."

I say, "Yes, he is wonderful," trying not to laugh out loud. Truly my husband is one of the kindest people on earth and he *is* so nice and wonderful, but what am I supposed to say in response to this gush? I'm not surprised that the support staff apparently has a collective, benign crush on my guy. It's just weird hearing him put on a pedestal of admiration, with me established in someone else's mind as the lucky woman who gets to share his pillow. I knew my love when he was a medical assistant who lived with his mom and preached at a Methodist church when the pastor was away. I would have been fine if he was a nurse, or an EMT, or a boat fixer, so long as he was himself, doing what gave him joy in a fruitful way. I'd have been fine with it. It so happens that the Great Physician has imprinted my love with a calling in medicine, and I love him for who he is, period. Which means that I love my man for the healing physician that has always on some level been a part of who is, waiting to be expressed, in spite of the arduous trip through medical education so that he can practice his calling. So whatever. My love is a human being with a calling to medicine, sexy enough without a pedestal. I'll tell you the truth: I'm happy we share pillows, among other things, but do not need to be treated like a special fabric. I'm just me. And my love is just him. Which suits us fine.

Soon the crowd thins as various conversations wind down, but the band is still playing strong. Several program faculty members are in the band, blowing air jovially into wind instruments. My love's dad, who is a doctor, also plays a wind instrument. Is there a connection between listening for breath sounds and creating them for pleasure? I wonder. I also wonder if my love is going to dance with me, after all, or if that intention will slip into the wind and dissipate into nothing. I'm not in the mood to force it tonight.

And just when I'm thinking the moment won't happen, it does.

My love gently grabs my arm and pulls me in the direction of the music.

In a whirl of toes happily stepping on each other, we merge with spontaneous spins and beginner swing steps out on the dance floor. With our own brand of improv, my love and I dance and dance and dance. The whole time we are laughing. Love is in the air and it's as if the band is playing just for us.

About the Author

Alicia Kwon is a healer, life coach, and founder of Awesome Alchemy with Alicia, a cutting-edge approach to helping families with unique needs and health issues find their way to wellness, love & joy. Alicia lives in Madison, Wisconsin, with her wonderful husband who is a family practice physician and their three amazing homeschooled children. Alicia can be found dancing in the clinic parking lot or the health food store checkout line, goofing off with her kids, at her office working with clients or with a good book under a shady tree. You can learn more or connect with Alicia online at www.aliciakwon.com.

**Here we are during my husband's
intern year, in and around Portland.**

**Ko was on-call Christmas eve, so we
had him come home as "Santa."**

**Here we are five years later on vacation on
the Big Island of Hawaii!**

Made in the USA
San Bernardino, CA
22 April 2015